For Golfers
and Other Athletes

For Golfers
and Other Athletes

by Dr. Wanita Holmes
with James Walter Caufield

BURMANBOOKS
.com

Copyright © 2005 Dr. Wanita Holmes

Published by BurmanBooks Inc.
4 Lamay Cres. Scarborough, Ontario Canada M1X 1J1

BURMANBOOKS
.com

All right reserved. No part of this publication may be reproduced,
stored in a retrieval system, or transmitted in any form by any process
– electronic, photocopying, recording, or otherwise –
without the prior written consent of BurmanBooks Inc.

Holmes, Dr. Wanita
The Inner Power Series For Golfers and Other Athletes/
Dr. Wanita Holmes

Cover Design by www.AliveDesign.com

Edited by Solidus Communications www.solidus.ca

Typesetting by TypeWorx

Distribution:

Canada: Jaguar Book Group,
    100 Armstrong Avenue
    Georgetown, Ontario L7G 5S4

United States: Independent Publishers Group,
    814 North Franklin Street,
    Chicago, Ill 60610

ISBN 0-9737166-1-4

Other Burman Books Available:

The Inner Power Series:

For Golfers and Other Athletes
Seducing Your Man
Intuitive Security for Women
Abundance for Life, Love and Money
Anxiety and Depression

Call Waiting (fiction)

You are always welcome to visit
www.BurmanBooks.com

A letter from the publisher

Dear Valued Reader;

The idea of The Inner Power Series came about after I spent some years in the film industry making movies like *Spider* with David Cronenberg, and TV shows like *Sidebar* on CBC Newsworld all by the time I was twenty-eight years of age. I decided to take some time off from the entertainment industry, since the more I accomplished the less happy I became.

Fate drew me to the authors who eventually wrote The Inner Power Series books. They were all very accomplished professionals who seemed to really enjoy life, earn great livings and yet stay grounded. Their stories, philosophies and accomplishments in helping other people inspired me to start the company and launch these books.

I knew I was on the right track, since all the other publishers turned me down (which generally is a great sign!), and from envisioning one that led to five in only four months, we have put together this special series.

I know you will notice the difference immediately after reading and learning the best techniques from the best teachers. We look forward to being your partners during your inner growth period. We want to help you accomplish your goals and achieve the greatness that is within you. Please write to us and let us know about your experiences after reading this book.

Yours truly,

Sanjay Burman
BurmanBooks Inc.

BurmanBooks.com

To Kristen,
without whom I could never have done this book.

To Chris,
who goaded me into doing this book.

To Linda and Mary,
for their constant support.

Acknowledgements

I am deeply grateful for seventy-six years of living and learning. I give thanks for the lessons that I have learned (some harsh and some sweet and gentle) that I can pass on to you.

I thank all my daughters for all their encouragement and for not only being my daughters, but for being my best friends.

I am incredibly grateful to Kris who put up with my tantrums, frustrations and impatience as I constantly made changes in the manuscript. I would like to thank Sanjay for his dreams, his courage and his ability to bring it all to fruition.

A special thanks to Jim Caufield who took all my fragmented stories and information and organized them into a book. And to Catherine my editor for her brilliance, her patience, her special talent for knowing what it takes to complete a manuscript i.e., book.

And a final thanks to all my athletes, students, clients and family who kept insisting that I write a book.

Table of Contents

	Page
Preface: Change Your Brain—Change Your Game	13

Part 1: The Spirit of the Game

Chapter 1: Welcome to the Magic	15
Chapter 2: Hypnosis and the Mysterious Brain	21
Chapter 3: Belief and Expectation	30

Part 2: Tee Here Now

Chapter 4: Taking Your Cue	36
Chapter 5: It's All in Your Head	42

Part 3: The Game of the Spirit

Chapter 6: And the Word Became Flesh	47
Chapter 7: Think Nothing. Feel Nothing. Be Nothing.	52
Chapter 8: Let Go. Let Golf.	61

Appendix A: Doing the Dirty Work	67
Appendix B: Breathing: The Breath of Life	87
Appendix C: Your Induction	89
Appendix D: Your Golf Script	97
Appendix E: Follow Your Bliss	101
Bibliographies	113

Preface:
Change Your Brain—Change Your Game

Read this book and *you* will lower your golf score. It's that simple. Does that surprise you? Maybe you thought *I would* lower your score *for* you. After all, I'm the licensed hypnotherapist with twenty years of clinical practice. I'm the one who conducts hypnotherapy lectures and symposia around the world. I'm the one who's helped thousands of people lose weight, stop smoking, overcome anxiety, depression and countless other challenges. I'm the one who's helped thousands of people attain a wide variety of personal goals. But no. The fact is *you* are going to do the dirty work, because you have the *power*.

But "dirty work" isn't quite what this little book involves. Far from it. "Dirty work" is a common phrase for a nuts-and-bolts, hands-on involvement in reality. It often denotes the difference between a merely abstract intellectual theory and a real-world practice. While my techniques do create real-world changes, they do *not* involve work. There's no drudgery here. To the contrary, these techniques involve *play*. After all, golf is a game and we're here to play! This book is *not* a manual of theory. No. It's *all* about practice, but practice in two different senses. Practice in the sense of time spent on a driving range or a par-three course, perfecting the physical mechanics of your golf game—there's no avoiding that kind of practice. But this book is also about practice in the sense of a spiritual practice, a joyful game of the spirit that leads the soul upward toward perfection. It's the combination of these two senses of practice that you will find in the following pages. By using the hypnotic techniques described here, your golf game will become relaxed, confident and well controlled. You'll *see* the shot you want to make and *make it*. The reality that you first create *inside* your mind will become a reality *outside* your mind, on the tee, on the fairway, on the green—and yes, even in your life as a whole. Sound easy? It is and you can make it so.

Hypnosis reduces stress, increases concentration and improves your performance in any area of your life. Yes, you can change your golf game by changing your brain and you can change your brain through hypnosis. And along the way to lowering your golf score, along with learning, perhaps for the first time, what the spirit of the game of golf truly entails, you will also find yourself playing more fully—joyfully, hopefully, honestly and faithfully—the game of the spirit.

Part 1:
The Spirit of the Game

Chapter 1:
Welcome to the Magic

Let me begin by putting all my cards on the table. I started playing golf on a whim when I was sixty-eight and immediately became hooked, so I encouraged three of my friends to take lessons with me. We arrived at the driving range without any clubs, balls, gloves or equipment. Fortunately, our coach had clubs we could use. She showed us how to grip the club, how to swing it like a pendulum and how to follow through. It seemed easy enough. Then she told us to get a bucket of balls and begin hitting them. I placed my ball, imagined it was my ex-husband's head, and whacked it as hard as I could. Whoa! That ball flew through the air and landed past the seventy-five yard marker. In that moment, I was hooked on golf. I am a woman, a professional hypnotherapist and a player of nowhere near scratch golf, but I can teach you how to improve your game.

"Now what in the world," you might be asking yourself (especially if you are one of the old-school, locker-room type of skeptical jocks I so often meet in my practice), "could this woman possibly teach *me* about golf? I have been playing the game for decades. I have subscribed to *Golf Digest* since college. This sweet old lady cannot tell me anything I don't already know." This happens to me almost every time. Golfers take one look at me and get an uptight mentality, arms crossed in front of their chest, rigid body, set face and attitude—lots of attitude. I establish right away that they are not here to learn the mechanics of golf from me. Instead, they are here to learn about the mental game of golf.

"Golf is a game of ease, but it isn't easy." This saying, so profoundly true, was brought home to me with particular force as I read a story in Jack Canfield and Mark Victor Hansen's *A Second Helping of Chicken Soup*. This story shows the powers of self-hypnosis and the visualizing mind more sublimely than any other account I have ever read.

Major James Nesmeth wanted to lower his golf score, but he was unable to go to the golf course for seven years, because that's how long he was a Vietnam prisoner of war. During his long captivity, Major Nesmeth decided he would play eighteen holes of golf in his mind every day. This practice of mental golf saved his sanity during his long ordeal and by using self-hypnosis and visualization, he unknowingly discovered an amazing technique, the same technique you will learn in this book.

After seven years of mentally playing golf every day, Major Nesmeth finally regained his freedom. The first time he played a round of real golf after all those years, and in spite of still being physically weak from his ordeal, he shot a seventy-four. He had dropped twenty strokes from his game!

An amazing accomplishment. Now *this* is truly the power of visualization, and hypnosis can put you in the mental state to make miracles like this happen. For most of us, our life and sanity does not depend on our ability to focus our attention and visualize the reality we desire. But Major Nesmeth's experience demonstrates that successful visualization can offer real redemption, even in the face of life's greatest challenges.

I have successfully used the techniques of relaxation and visualization thousands of times, not only with golfers, but with other athletes, with actors, trial lawyers, test takers and many others.

In fact, anyone who's facing a grueling situation—a period of anxiety, stress, tension or pressure—can benefit enormously from the power of hypnosis and, given the prevailing mental climate of our modern world, that means just about everybody.

The approach in this book is simple. First, I will introduce some elementary facts about hypnosis and the brain, which will orient you to trance phenomena. Having a working knowledge of some of the basic concepts of hypnosis will make the application to your golf game even easier. Then we'll hit the first tee, apply our knowledge of hypnosis to the game of golf and watch the magic happen.

What is Hypnosis?

When it comes to hypnosis, generations of stage hypnotists and movie makers have left in the popular imagination a lingering concept of circus foolery, so it might be useful to make clear just what hypnosis is *not*. Hypnosis is not mind control. There's no danger that you'll get permanently stuck in a hypnotic trance and live out the balance of your life as a mindless zombie. You don't forfeit your own will when you enter a trance state. No one has ever performed any action while hypnotized that he would not as readily have done under normal circumstances.

We know that the ancient Egyptians used hypnosis very much as we do today, except we no longer wave crystals or diamonds or a gold watch in front of your face. Nor must you stare at a spinning spiral. This is more Hollywood mythologizing. These methods were indeed once used to bring on eye fatigue and then eye closure, but some clever hypnotist in the 1920s thought to say simply, "Please close your eyes," and the client did. This has been the standard procedure ever since.

Medical hypnosis has been used as a form of anesthesia for more than a century. Mysterious as it seems, hypnosis is so powerful that surgery can be performed on hypnotized patients who are allergic to normal anesthesia and they won't feel any pain. I had an hour-and-a-half surgery three years ago under hypnosis. When it was finished, I sat up on the operating table and said, "I'm hungry, let's go eat," and we did! No anesthesia, no long hospital stay, no recovery room and no post-surgical pain medication.

The doctor was amazed and so was I. I had pre-hypnotized myself for several weeks. I made a hypnosis tape and played it throughout the surgery. I was aware, but off in my own dream state. While very few doctors would be willing to operate on a hypnotized patient, you can always take a hypnosis tape into surgery and it will make the procedure easier.

The American Medical Association gave its stamp of approval to surgical hypnosis in 1958, and the first surgery done under AMA auspices was a thyroidectomy. The hypnotized patient was awake throughout the procedure but felt no pain. Hypnosis has been accepted as a viable substitute for anesthesia ever since. O ye of little faith, if the AMA isn't legit, what is?

Hypnotic trances have always played a part in the religious and mystical ceremonies of human societies. You need only think of the rhythmic drumming of African tribesmen or the monotone chanting of Himalayan holy men to recognize the importance of trance states. Analogues to these practices are found in many cultures around the world. Sufi enthusiasts, Catholic pietists, Native American shamans and Pacific Island witch doctors are all, in their various ways, inducing in themselves and others a hypnotic trance. Hypnosis is an ancient technique for altering the normal waking mental state.

At the same time, hypnosis is not simply meditation, though the two are akin. In meditation, the meditative state is itself the goal, but in hypnosis you enter a meditative state and then do some work on yourself to actively change the mental basis of your behavior. For centuries, Indian yogis have known how to

Chapter 1 - Welcome to the Magic

radically alter their states of mind and body. For instance, in one experiment a yogi was placed in a coffin-like enclosure. Researchers then lit a four-hour candle and placed it in the box with the yogi. When they opened it eight hours later, they found the candle was still burning. How could this happen? The yogi had put himself into a delta state—more on this term later—in which he was using just enough oxygen to keep himself alive. It's as though he were in hibernation. If they put me in that box, I suspect the candle would be used up in about twenty minutes, but the point is this: we don't know exactly how the mind controls the body, but something profoundly powerful is at work. That much is certain.

The modern, Western, scientific development of hypnosis is a much shorter story. The German psychiatrist Franz Mesmer stumbled upon the power of hypnotic suggestion in the mid-1700s. Because of Mesmer's research, the original term for hypnosis was mesmerism. Mesmer used an odd mixture of séances, harmonic therapy and theories of animal magnetism. It was left to other researchers, however, to discern that the apparent cures effected by Mesmer were in fact brought about by the power of suggestions made to patients while they were in a trance.

Further developing these ideas and techniques, James Braid (1795-1860), a Scottish surgeon, eventually coined the term hypnosis for the trance state. Braid derived his term from *hypnos*, the Greek word for sleep, because he supposed that his patients were entering a state of reduced awareness, literally falling asleep, but later concluded that patients were actually going into trance, which he then correctly recognized as a *heightened* state of awareness. This crucial quality of the trance state—its super-consciousness or heightened awareness—is central to its importance in changing behavior, such as improving your golf game.

As you can see, hypnosis enables you to use and maximize the power of your sub-conscious mind. It allows you to achieve your desires by changing your focus to success rather than failure. Using hypnosis to eradicate negative, self-defeating thoughts will help you play the game of golf you love and play it more powerfully and confidently.

Chapter 2:
Hypnosis and the Mysterious Brain

All hypnosis is at root self-hypnosis. It's a perfectly normal, natural state. Let me explain. Thanks to modern technology, the brain's electrical activity can be observed and measured by means of an electroencephalogram (EEG). You have probably heard of the common names of brainwave patterns, alpha, beta, theta and delta waves. EEG technology first revealed these energy levels of the brain in the mid-twentieth century. In hypnosis, we work with three of these energy levels, alpha, theta and delta.

Right now, as I write this and as you are reading, our brains are in the beta-wave range. This means we are alert and producing brainwaves at a rate of approximately forty energy units per second. In the beta state, the consciousness is totally scattered and diffuse, which is our normal waking state of mind. In this sense, we are all scatter-brained, and it's a good thing. We have a lot on our minds in this hectic world, like a juggler with five balls in the air, and the beta state typifies the daytime brain at its multitasking finest. In the beta state, we are not totally focused and concentrating on any one thing. For example, as I write this chapter, I am also watching the time, hearing the sounds outside, thinking about my next client, her problem, and how I'm going to work with her, wondering if my little dog, Attila, needs to go for a walk, etc. ad infinitum. All this is going on while I'm writing these words, and you could easily describe a similar state of consciousness as you read them. When you are in the beta state, your brainwaves are very active, as they should be.

The alpha state, on the other hand, is where the magic happens. Alpha is the brain's learning place and healing place. It is totally focused, and that's where hypnosis takes you. The alpha state is like a juggler with just one ball, and he is holding it in his hand, staring at it intently. When you undergo hypnosis, your brainwaves begin to slow down and enter the alpha state, with an energy output of approximately ten to fourteen energy units per second. You begin to feel very relaxed as your focus narrows. As this takes place, you are able to focus and concentrate one hundred percent.

As the hypnotic trance deepens, people sometimes automatically drift into the theta range, producing seven to ten units of electrical energy per second. This often happens to people who took drugs in their youth. It seems they are used to just letting go. In this sense, former drug use actually makes one a good candidate for hypnosis. Their attitude is one of curiosity and experimentation, however, I do not recommend the use of drugs.

The occasional client even experiences the delta range, producing a mere four to seven units of electricity per second. This is called the somnambulistic state. If you were about to undergo surgery, I would put you into the delta range, though this deep-trance state is not necessary for our present purposes. When you're in delta, you might feel as though you're asleep. You might even snore, but you won't be asleep in the usual sense of that word. In fact, when listening to their taped sessions, people often ask, "Who is that snoring on the tape?" I always laugh and say, "Well, there were just the two of us here and I was talking, so who do you think was snoring?"

Returning to the alpha state, let me repeat that hypnosis is a naturally occurring event in each of our lives. We enter the alpha state for two or three hours every day, but we don't need a hypnotherapist to take us there. In fact, it's as natural as falling asleep. When you go to sleep, you pass through what is called a hypnagogic state, which simply means a state leading to sleep. You are transitioning from wakefulness to sleep. The parasympathetic nervous system is shutting down and the sympathetic nervous system is taking over, preparing to keep your lungs breathing, your blood circulating and your heart beating whether for a solid eight hours of shuteye or a quick catnap. In this hypnagogic state, you are neither wholly awake, nor wholly asleep, nor are you yet dreaming. The same thing happens in reverse when you awaken, and of course the professionals have given it an equally fancy name: the hypnopompic state.

As you may know from your own experience, a variety of vivid, dreamlike auditory and visual hallucinations can occur during these sleep-transition phases. Whatever the ultimate source of these sensations, an EEG reveals that the pattern of brainwave activity found in these transitional states is identical to that of a person in a hypnotic trance. Basically, in the passage from waking to sleeping, the brain automatically cycles down from the beta range into the alpha range. Hypnosis manipulates this natural mechanism of the brain, causing the same down-cycling into the alpha range, but without the person going to sleep. To repeat, the alpha state is characterized by a profoundly deep relaxation of the body and a narrowing of your focus. The sub-conscious mind is then receptive to constructive suggestions, which we will have discussed during the interview.

The Thinking Mind and the Action Mind

Duality is of the essence of the human condition. This truism is repeated in many different ways and at many different times. It seems that each of us must learn this. One basic duality appears in the distinction between the mind and the body. The mind and body are fundamentally one. Their unity is discernible in many ways, not least on a golf course. A second traditional duality is positioned within the mind itself and is expressed, in modern terms, sometimes as the right-brain and left-brain split, sometimes as the intuitive and analytical halves of the mind. These are names for the same phenomenon. I personally prefer to use the mental division of the *thinking mind* and the *action mind*.

The thinking mind is the conscious mind. It thinks the thoughts and the action mind carries them out. Many of my male clients are so thoroughly dominated by their left brain, that they ignore the importance of their right brain. The right brain is the intuitive and emotional part of the brain. The thinking mind, the conscious, does not take suggestions. It is like a lost motorist who won't stop and ask for directions. The conscious mind is built for thinking. It likes what it knows and does not look much beyond its own limits. It is also sometimes a control freak. The thinking conscious mind is extremely reluctant to relinquish control. It can sometimes be so resistant to relaxation that it spoils the joys of life. This person with left-brain dominance is not interested in emotions and intuition. The thinking conscious mind is often unwilling to loosen its grip at all. This suggests that to let go at all is to let go wholly, even unto death. We will return to the thinking mind later, but now we will look at the action mind.

The action mind is the sub-conscious mind. It is an obedient servant who does not think or reason. It just follows orders, and these orders come from the thinking mind. The action mind cannot tell fantasy from reality. It just does what it's told, and this is why hypnosis has such a tremendously powerful effect on the mind. Through hypnosis, you can give constructive suggestions directly to the action mind, which will accept these suggestions and cause them to become reality. Although we don't know exactly how or why this works, there's no doubt that it does work. By giving new marching orders directly to the sub-conscious action mind, we can circumvent many of the faulty and negative suggestions given by the thinking conscious mind.

The thinking mind often gives the action mind the wrong suggestions or instructions and, as it does not know a good order from a bad one, the action mind accepts what it is given and acts

Chapter 2 - Hypnosis and the Mysterious Brain

accordingly. The action mind has no morals, no sense of humor, no discrimination. Therefore when the thinking mind says, "Do *not* hit the ball into the sand trap," the action mind hears only the words, "Hit the ball into the sand trap," and it directs the body accordingly, with the result that you end up in the trap. The "Do *not*" part of the statement is completely lost. Here is another example: if I say to you "Don't think of an elephant," what do you think of? If I say to you, "Don't think of a martini glass," I know that is what you thought of! Elementary school teachers are well aware of the importance of this trait in children. Directions to young children must always be stated positively. Negative statements are lost on the action mind, which predominates in childhood.

Be aware then, that when you are in a hypnotic state, you are directly accessing your sub-conscious mind, your action mind. It's your best friend and it will always do what you tell it to do. Your thinking mind thinks the thought and your action mind acts it out. Imagine your thinking mind as a camera and your action mind as the film. The film can only produce the picture the camera has taken. It cannot change it. The sub-conscious mind does not know the difference between fantasy and reality. Remember, it has no sense of humor, no morals, no judgments—it does only what the thinking mind tells it to do. Given the character of relations between the thinking and action minds, what is the upshot? Simply this: You are what you think. You cannot escape it. Two thousand years ago, in the bible, it was written, "As a man thinketh, so shall he Be." It also was written, "The word becomes the flesh." Today, we simply say, "You are what you think." It was right two thousand years ago and it's right today.

The literature of hypnosis abounds with illustrations of this deep truth. For example, a mother sees her child trapped under a car. She weighs 125 pounds and the car weighs 3,000 pounds. In spite of this brute fact, she races over, picks up the car and frees her child without hurting herself. Why? How? Easy. She simply *sees* herself able to do it and does it. Remember, what the mind can conceive, the body can achieve. Imagine a similar accident where the mother screams, "Oh! My baby! Help! My baby!" She will never be able to lift the car, because she cannot *see* herself doing it. She believes she cannot.

"Listen to the sound of my voice..."

There are also interesting examples from my own practice and from other hypnosis studies, that I would like to share with you. In the first place, please recall that you are not asleep when under hypnosis. You might feel like you are asleep and you might even snore. At least sixty percent of my clients do snore. It's perfectly normal. To an outside observer, who does not know anything about hypnosis, you would look like you are asleep. If someone were to come into my office during a hypnotherapy session, he would probably say, "Oh, I'm sorry. I didn't know someone was sleeping in here." My hypnotized client would probably even hear this intruder, but would feel so euphoric and so relaxed that she wouldn't even open her eyes. But as we know, even though you look like you are asleep, your mind is in fact more focused, more centered and more concentrated than at any other time. Several times, I have had clients under hypnosis when an earthquake aftershock happened to occur. While I was barely forming the thought, "Oh my God, an earthquake!" my client was already up, alert and ready to move.

Some clients can hear when under hypnosis, but others do not. At least ten percent of my clients, in their initial session, hear everything I say. That does not mean they are not hypnotized. It means they are simply nosey or control-conscious people. I often find that people in positions of authority, such as engineers, teachers and policeman, often hear everything and that is just fine.

Chapter 2 - Hypnosis and the Mysterious Brain

Another twenty percent *think* they have heard everything I said during the session. To them I always say, "Well, good. That's great," even when I'm sure they haven't really heard everything. And when they come back for their next appointment, they say sheepishly, "Wanita, I listened to my tape. You know, I hardly heard anything you said. Where was I?"

Yet another ten percent have complete audio amnesia. After about five sentences, their conscious mind stops listening, but their sub-conscious mind is taking it all in. And that's just fine.

The remaining clients just seem to go tripping off to some place of their own. They hear some of what I say and then drift away, sometimes seeing colors, hearing music, working on problems, then my voice slowly comes back to their awareness and they think they had better listen. I tell them, "You don't have to listen. Just trust yourself. Your sub-conscious mind is always listening. Know that whatever you do will be just right for you."

And even after I have explained all this to my clients, some will persist in saying, "I don't think I was really hypnotized. You know, I heard everything you said," or "I think I must have fallen asleep, because I didn't hear a word you said." When it comes to your own hypnotic experiences, just remember that there is no right or wrong way to experience hypnosis. Just sit back and relax and let the magic happen.

You will learn much more about the strange processes of the thinking and the action minds and the astounding power of hypnosis, and you will see what an immense influence this can have on your golf game or anything else you may wish to change. I would like to share with you several changes I have made in my own life with the use of hypnosis and how applicable these types of changes can be for your golf game.

Conquering Challenges and Fears On and Off the Golf Course

I have improved my golf game, had surgery and even had a tooth pulled while using hypnosis. I have also conquered lifetime fears. I know that what I have done, you can do to. Hypnosis can change any area of your life, not just golf.

From the time I was a little girl, I had been morbidly afraid of heights. I could not even stand near a window above the third floor without breaking into a sweat. When I went to the Grand Canyon, I could not go near the edge. People were throwing rocks and waiting to see how long it would take to hear the sound of their rock landing on the canyon floor. Just the thought made me queasy.

Soon after I started doing hypnosis, I was invited to go hot-air ballooning. My immediate response was thanks, but no thanks! Then the idea that I could use hypnosis to rid myself of this fear compelled me to call my friend and say, "I'd love to go!" I had a week to work on myself. I made a hypnosis tape and listened to it, over and over again. By Sunday morning, I was ready. What an experience! What a feeling to be free of a life-long fear. I loved flying in that balloon. That one experience totally freed me of my fear.

After that, I went up one-hundred-and-ten floors in the World Trade Center without the slightest shred of the old fear. I am thinking of jumping out of a plane when I'm eighty. I used to say, if my plane was going down, even if I had a parachute, I would choose to stay on the plane. Not any more! Just think, if hypnosis can get rid of this fear, it will be easy to let go of any fear or anxiety on the golf course!

Another fear I had was of dancing. I know this doesn't seem like a big deal, but it was! I would go out with my friends when they went dancing and I would just sit and watch. I longed to be able to dance, but I was too fearful of having people watching me on the dance floor. I broke many men's hearts. They would ask me to dance and I would say, "No thank you, I don't dance." I even passed up a date with Gene Kelly because I was afraid he would ask me to dance. Once, I went out on a blind date with a famous director. We had dinner and then the band began to play. He asked me to dance, but when I said, "I don't dance," he insisted. We got up and after one turn around the dance floor, he maneuvered me back to the table. After we sat down, he laughed and said, "God, you really can't dance!"

When I was sixty-five, I decided I was not going to leave this planet before I learned to dance. I started taking ballroom dance lessons. On the fourth lesson, I started laughing and said to my instructor, "No wonder I couldn't dance. I never had a clue how to do it!"

After six months of lessons and daily hypnosis regarding the joy and freedom of dancing, I did an exhibition dance in front of two hundred people. I am not Terpsichore, the goddess of dance, but I can dance!

The wonderful thing I discovered was that people were not watching me or judging me on the dance floor. I realized you have to be either very good or simply awful before they even look at you.

Is this not applicable to your golf game? Everyone is more interested in his own shot, his own drive, his own putt, than yours. Unless you are a spectacular player, a Tiger Woods, Ernie Els or Vijay Singh, or you lose your cool and hit a spectacularly lousy shot, chances are no one is watching. Even then, other golfers are generally sympathetic, because they have experienced the same problems.

Remember: you are what you think—the words you speak, the words you hear, the words you think. Create who you are!

Chapter 3:
Belief and Expectation

I have been doing hypnosis for eighteen years. I have done sessions for everything you can imagine. My typical routine with new clients is to begin with an in-depth interview. Whether they have come for help with their golf game, tennis, basketball or any other issue, I first find out something about my clients, because this can assist immensely in the healing process. I try to get a sense of their character, their personality type and their general situation in life. I also check out their attitude toward hypnosis and if necessary, dispel any fears, any misconceptions, and any Hollywood myths that might lurk in their imaginations.

The basic formula for successful hypnosis is simple and can be reduced to two core ideas: *belief* and *expectation*. When I speak to people on the phone, by the time we're done talking, they truly understand that whatever they want to change in their lives, is going to happen. This is the belief factor. By the time they walk through my door, fifty percent of my work is done. As they already expect results from hypnosis, they get results. Belief and expectation are the tools for successful hypnotherapy. I also explain to new clients that hypnosis is simply deep relaxation and a narrowing down of their focus.

What Works for You?

What happens in a hypnotherapy session? When working with a golfer, I first have them tell me about their game. What do they think are their particular strengths? Where does their game need to improve? What brought them to see me? I ask them to describe in detail the very best round of golf they have ever played.

Chapter 3 - Belief and Expectation

Typical questions include:
- Who were you playing with?
- Where did you play?
- What were you wearing?
- Were you wearing any significant garments, such as new shoes or a particular shirt or hat?
- What was the weather like?
- What were the circumstances?
- Were you on vacation?
- Were you playing with a new set of clubs?
- Were you on a course that was new to you?
- Were you gambling on the game?

I then ask clients to stand up and show me their swing. Now I'm not a professional golf instructor, of course, but I can make some general observations about the fundamentals of a golf swing, such as whether one's knees are slightly bent, whether the follow-through is complete, if the head is up, if the general posture appears correct, whether the swing is relaxed and the manner of one's breathing. I ask my clients whether they have ever taken golf lessons and if so, what their pro's particular instructions and criticisms were. If I'm working with a professional golfer, I ask:
- How do you cope with crowds?
- How do you handle being watched on every play?
- How do you feel about the presence and scrutiny of TV cameras and crews?

Finally, I ask all my clients to describe how they react to a less-than-perfect shot. Does their predominant reaction involve feelings of anger, embarrassment, resignation? Or are they more apt to respond by thinking, mulling over the imperfect shot and calculating and analyzing the minutia of swing mechanics?

This basic information will prove very valuable when it comes to making post-hypnotic suggestions.

Relax, Close Your Eyes, Take A Deep Breath...

The alpha state, this daydreamy state of mind, occurs naturally when people meditate, listen to music, watch movies or television, drive on a highway at night, or perform a repetitious task. Have you ever found that you have left work intending to go by the post office and then suddenly found yourself parked at home? Your conscious mind took a little holiday. Driving is an activity especially conducive to a mild trance state. Whether the hypnosis is done in a hypnotherapist's office or is self-induced, the trance state fosters a shift in the sub-conscious mind.

This is how I proceed in my practice. I ask my clients to take off their shoes, their glasses, turn off their cell phone and move over to my big comfy chair. I cover them with a blanket, put on a headset, cover their eyes and start playing soothing music. Next, I instruct them to focus inwardly and to take a deep relaxing breath, inhaling very slowly, holding it in for a few seconds and then exhaling very slowly. Now take another deep breath, breathing from the bottom up. Breathe so that your tummy seems to fill up and expand, then your upper chest and lungs fill up. (In Yoga, this is called diaphragmatic breathing.) Now exhale very slowly, allowing your tummy to relax. This breathing might seem a little tricky at first, but you do not need to focus too closely on it or try too hard. The idea is simply to take slow, deep breaths in whatever way is most comfortable for you. Inhale slowly through your nose. Hold the air in your lungs for a moment and then exhale slowly through your mouth, which should be slightly open. Again, do not fixate on these details of breathing. Just get comfortable and breathe slowly and deeply. You will feel your body relaxing with each breath. As you continue to breathe, you will feel your body relax more and more.

Chapter 3 - Belief and Expectation

You're now on your way into a hypnotic trance. At this point in the session, I begin the induction. You will find an induction in Appendix C. I suggest you to read it now. Eventually, you might choose to make a tape recording of this induction and the Golf Script in Appendix D for yourself, or you can purchase CDs or tapes from me directly. Ordering information is given in the back of this book.

I have done more than forty thousand hypnotic sessions and I know that inductions bring a calm, clear, focused state of mind. This is the magical alpha state, which side-steps the thinking mind and permits constructive suggestions to be anchored in your action mind. These sub-conscious suggestions will dramatically improve your golf game and your life.

As you can see even from this brief description, hypnosis allows you to relax very deeply and thoroughly. That's the first thing you will notice. When you are deeply relaxed, you can hear better, listen more intently. When you listen more intently to what I say to you under hypnosis, it will sink in better. When it sinks in on a deeper level, you will respond better to the post-hypnotic suggestions. This in turn allows a greater awareness. You will be in a super-alert state while under hypnosis. Many uninformed people think that because you are snoring while hypnotized, that you are asleep. In fact, the brain is extremely aware and alert when in a hypnotic trance. I don't mean alert in the sense that your body is tense with watchfulness, as if adrenaline were coursing through your veins and your ears were pricked up, like a dog on point. Far from it. The body's muscles, organs, tissues and nerves are totally relaxed and only the brain is in a state of maximum receptivity. Here's another story to illustrate the power of hypnosis and how suggestions affect your behavior and your golf game.

Professor Ernest Hilgard, who founded the Stanford University Laboratory of Hypnosis in 1957, was conducting research with a group of students. They hypnotized a certifiably blind student named John and made him temporarily deaf, a phenomenon termed audio amnesia. The researchers shot a gun, turned on the fire alarm, blared loud music, screamed and shouted, but found absolutely no response from the subject, who was wired up with electrodes to register even the slightest audio response. Nothing happened!

Then one of the students said, "Professor Hilgard, this man is not deaf. He walked in here and he could hear. He has got to be able to hear somewhere."

Professor Hilgard then said to the subject, "John, if you can hear me anywhere, please lift the index finger on your right hand."

As they waited, John's finger slowly rose. When they brought John out of hypnosis, they asked him what it was like. "Being blind can sometimes be pretty boring," he said, "but being deaf *and* blind is very boring. But you know, one funny thing did happen. I felt my index finger go up for no reason at all."

When you use this same technique while playing golf, shooting baskets or playing tennis, you will be able to narrow your focus to concentrate completely.

Further research allowed investigators to discover that even when a patient is under anesthesia, she can still hear. This has changed the behavior in operating rooms. Doctors and nurses are now much more careful about what they say and the music they play. During surgery, the doctor will now tell his patient how well she's doing and sometimes even encourage the patient to control her own bleeding. And she can and does! This remarkable ability to slow bleeding, control blood pressure, tune out sounds and regulate heartbeat indicates the awesome power of your mind.

Chapter 3 - Belief and Expectation

If you use just a little of this power on the golf course, you can put yourself in the now and be present. You can shut out anything that disturbs or distract you when you are going for that million-dollar putt. Then you can slow down your breathing, slow down your heartbeat, steady yourself, take your time and sink it. There is no sweeter sound than the sound of the ball going in the cup!

Part 2:
Tee Here Now

Chapter 4:
Taking Your Cue

If you look past the silly pun in this section's title, you might just get an immediate, intuitive sense of what hypnosis can do for you and your golf game. Once you experience the profound calm and focused clarity of the alpha state and learn how to take yourself to that place at will, you will know that the real secret of golf hypnosis lies in empowering yourself to maintain expansive vision, effortless focus, abundant confidence, a feeling of timelessness, and a complete freedom from anxiety and doubt. After all, golf is a game that is played largely between the ears.

If you ask any player, amateur or professional, what fraction of her game is mental, she will tell you that the mental side accounts for at least eighty percent, once all the rudimentary skills have been learned. Yet while golfers spend countless hours practicing, taking lessons and reading books to learn how to improve their swing or their putting stroke, they rarely spend any time at all working on improving their mental skills. If golf is such a mental game, why do players spend so much of their time, energy—and money!—on swing mechanics instead of brain mechanics? I think the answer to this question is the same as the answer to why all the golf books, videos, magazines and coaches on the market are equally negligent of golf's inner game. Many are aware of the overwhelming importance of golf's psychological dimension, but for many of them it is not their area of expertise. They have no map for that territory and are leery of venturing beyond their own personal knowledge of the game. That's the thinking mind's fear of the new, the unknown, and it's also why the hypnotic techniques I offer have such a marvelous effect. You change your brain and change you game.

But I have yet to mention the biggest gain for your golf game that hypnosis brings: it will teach you how to get into the super-focused alpha state before *every single shot*. You simply give your action mind the order to relax and you do it before each stroke. How do you accomplish this? The process is easy once you are accustomed to the trance state. First, before entering the trance, you choose some action that you are comfortable doing while on the golf course, some small thing that you might do before hitting the ball. This can be as simple as wiping your clubhead, adjusting the Velcro fastener on your golf glove, taking off your hat and running your fingers through your hair, saying some particular word or phrase, or inwardly singing or humming a snatch of a song—any fairly brief and unobtrusive action will do. The possibilities are endless.

It's been said that Ben Hogan always hummed the tune "Edelweiss" before hitting a shot. Personally, I sing "Up, Up and Away" to myself; it seems especially fitting for a golf drive. The action you choose becomes your *cue*. This cue produces a reaction to a post-hypnotic suggestion that was planted in your subconscious mind, your action mind, during a trance. Once this post-hypnotic suggestion is embedded in your action mind, then every time you give yourself your particular cue, you will immediately enter the alpha state of deep relaxation and super-alertness. Your handicap will soon show the difference!

A Hypnotic Cue is not a Pre-shot Routine

Some sports psychologists teach similar relaxation exercises, though these usually lack the inner power that hypnosis provides. For instance, the use of a cue is similar to the common activity golfers call a "pre-shot routine," but the differences are important.

The pre-shot routine is a precisely scripted and invariable set of actions you perform before each shot. A typical pre-shot routine might involve first standing behind your ball and picking a target to aim at, then approaching your ball, placing the clubhead, placing your right foot, then your left, looking at the target, waggling once, looking at the target, waggling again and then swinging. The idea is that if you do the same series of things over and over in a robotic fashion, whether on the driving range or on the course, then your *body* will eventually have a very difficult time discerning the difference between a high-pressure situation and a zero-pressure, driving-range situation. Some advocates of the pre-shot routine even suggest that you observe it faithfully, using it every single time you hit a ball—anywhere, any shot. Others advise using it only once every five shots on the driving range and before each and every shot on the course.

The big difference between a post-hypnotic cue and the pre-shot routine is the pre-shot's tendency to aggravate the conscious mind. The main benefit you derive from hypnosis is relaxation. Many players are so firmly fixated on their mechanics—Is my left arm straight? Is my elbow tucked? I must stay level with the swing plane. I must rotate my hips in the follow-through, etc.—that they never really fully swing, because their head is full of tips and pointers and lessons. The one thing hypnosis does best is teach the golfer to stay very, very relaxed or, if he should start to feel tension building up, to begin taking three deep breaths, as explained in Appendix B, and using whatever he has chosen as a cue to induce the alpha state of focused relaxation. The breathing oxygenates the brain and relaxes the muscles. Your brain weighs three pounds and uses one third of the oxygen you take in. Slow, deep breaths fill your brain and muscles with the oxygen you need to have them function at your highest capabilities. The pre-shot routine, however, simply adds another layer of mechanical complexity to an already overwrought thinking mind, so that along with worrying about the swing mechanics, the tense golfer now has an additional checklist of dos and don'ts to obsess over. Was that one waggle or two? Did I wipe my clubhead before putting on my glove or after? Did I pick my intermediate target before addressing the ball? Did I tug my left earlobe before my right? You see the problem. Once your pre-shot routine becomes completely ritualized, then perhaps the thinking mind is helped to relax and fall silent, but this can take a long time. We will explore this problem in more detail later, but for now I'll simply say that a firmly rooted post-hypnotic suggestion, one that automatically triggers the alpha state of deep relaxation, can bring about this goal immediately and without any elaborate ritual apparatus.

Golfers agree the pre-shot routine shows that concentration is crucial in golf and the most minute distraction, such as someone coughing, the click or the flash of a camera, someone clearing his throat or planes overhead can have a major effect on focus and concentration.

The Lie and the Lay of the Land

Chris, a young golfer I worked with, would always play two or three balls at a time, and of these he would always play the best lie. You have no doubt seen golfers play this way on your local course. Chris came to me because his game simply would not improve. He couldn't break 100 no matter what he tried. "You are confusing the ball," I told him. "Your *intention* is getting diluted." We talked about alternative strategies. After several session of hypnosis, Chris started playing only one ball per hole and he became scrupulous in keeping score. He began counting every stroke and playing only one ball, and soon, he broke 100 for the first time. All it took was one ball, counting every stroke, to finally break one hundred! It seems the golf gods finally began to smile on him, for now he shoots in the low eighties consistently.

Honesty has its rewards on the golf course. Study the lay of the course and let go of the lies on the course.

Visualization for a Winning Edge

Okay, now that you've learned some of the ABCs of hypnosis and how hypnosis is induced, we're just about ready to apply hypnosis to the game of golf. You remember Major Nesmeth, the Vietnam POW who saved his sanity by painstakingly visualizing a round of golf every day for seven years? Then you know that self-hypnosis can, in extreme circumstances, have truly remarkable power. Let us consider some more mundane examples of this power drawn from the world of sports.

First, I would like to look at the findings of sports psychologists in the former Soviet Union, who over the last half of the twentieth century regularly used hypnosis with their Olympic athletes. For example, during tryouts for their Olympic basketball team, they divided thirty potential players into three groups. The first group practiced actually shooting free throws for one hour a day. The second group practiced free throws for thirty minutes and then spent another thirty minutes using hypnosis and visualizing their free throws mentally. The third group spent the full hour under hypnosis, visualizing their free throws one right after another, with the guidance of their hypnotherapist. At the end of twenty-one days, they all took the court to practice free throws. Who do you think performed best? The ones who used hypnosis and visualization for the full hour. When they visualized their intentions, they never saw themselves miss. They approached the free throw line with high expectations and very low apprehension, once again proving that you are what you think.

Another interesting experiment the Russians did was wiring their athletes with electrodes and then putting them into a deep hypnotic state. The athletes were instructed to picture themselves doing their Olympic sport, whether it was ice-skating, weight lifting, gymnastics, swimming, diving, etc. The researchers discovered that those muscles the athletes would normally use when actually engaged in their sports were emitting electrical energy, even though they were lying absolutely still in an hypnotic state. This clearly showed that thoughts have energy. The athletes were electrically engaging those crucial muscles by simply imagining themselves performing. The word really does become the flesh.

Chapter 5:
It's All in Your Head

I have used these techniques successfully with many golfers, as well as actors, law students taking the bar exam, public speakers and a host of others. In fact, anyone facing a stressful situation stands to benefit from hypnosis. Along with your alpha-state cue, the three deep, relaxing breaths (see Appendix B) help to calm the mind, bring oxygen to the brain, and *focus* the attention wholly on a single object. The process is simple and the results can be tremendous, so why haven't more golfers caught on to hypnosis?

Let's learn from this story of Tom.

Something Outside Your Game is the Problem

Tom was a long-drive powerhouse, but he never won in competitive tournaments. Here was a man who could hit a golf ball 350 yards at a driving range, but whose power drive fell apart when the heat was on. His wife, who was concerned by his chronic struggle and frustration with his game, referred him to me.

Tom and I got off on the wrong foot. We were scheduled to meet at 2:00 p.m., but I was kept a few minutes longer than expected with another client. When I checked my waiting room, it was empty. He told my receptionist he could not wait any longer. I knew very well that Tom was a man of the leisure who did nothing but play golf. What could possibly make him so angry that he would walk out and leave simply because I was a few minutes late? Hmmm, something didn't quite add up.

My first inclination was to forget about him. After all, people generally know more about what they need than their therapists do, so if someone declines a hypnotherapy session, I find it wise to abide by their wishes. My thriving practice does not lack for

Chapter 5 - It's All in Your Head

sufficient clientele. People come to me from all over the world to be hypnotized and one client more or less is no great matter to me. Still, when I thought of Tom's wife's concerns when she described his problem to me, my compassion overrode my reluctance to call him. So I called him, apologized for keeping him waiting and encouraged him to reschedule the appointment, assuring him that I could certainly help him.

When Tom returned for his appointment, he sat down in my comfy office chair, crossed his arms and legs and glowered at me from under his brows with a look that indicated to me that he was very skeptical of me and of hypnosis. His attitude and body language made that perfectly clear.

I just smiled at him and said, "I know what you are thinking." His face turned beet red as he squirmed uncomfortably in his chair. I said, "You are wondering what the heck I can teach you about golf." He smiled slightly. I told him, "I don't play golf." (I had not yet started). "I do not know a putter from an iron. In fact if I think of an iron, it's something you use to press clothes. But Tom, you know how to play golf and how to be the long-drive champion. What I am going to be doing here today is finding out what is interfering with your ability to be a champion. Then I am going to do hypnosis to empower you, allowing you to be a winner!"

Well, it took some doing, but Tom and I eventually established a very productive rapport. His situation was one I frequently see in male clients. Tom had a father complex. I don't mean this is any deep, dark, Freudian sense, though of course the roots of our emotional relations to our parents do extend to the foundation of our personalities and often play a significant role in our adult lives.

The facts were these: Tom and his father often played golf together. His father was perhaps his most enthusiastic fan and Tom always told his father when he was playing in a long drive tournament. His father always attended these events. Deep down, Tom didn't feel comfortable with being better than his father at long-ball driving or at *anything*, ultimately, but that is a longer story. He didn't want to make his father feel bad by being better than him. We discovered it was his father's presence at tournaments that seemed to cause Tom's confidence to fall apart. All these feelings were gradually revealed during our session. I told Tom the solution for this problem was simple: leave your father home. Do not tell him when you are competing. Tom smiled a big grin and agreed to try this. The upshot is described below.

Tom also had trouble with the gallery and the media at his tournaments. As with many of us, inspection made him extremely self-conscious. This is another very common rough spot for golfers, whether we are just playing or competing in a tournament. Our ambition and our fear are locked in a permanent struggle. We desperately wish to do well, to look good, to be admired and at the same time, we're petrified that we will do poorly, look foolish and incompetent, and earn scorn and contempt. Yes, we're all drama queens at heart.

For Tom, the glare of the spotlights and the continual, intense scrutiny by the crowds made him freeze up. He would breathe very shallowly, depriving his muscles of oxygen so they would tighten up. With hypnosis, the beta state and its constant chatter fades out entirely. The alpha state fosters a calm relaxed state. I worked with Tom on focusing his concentration, silencing the conscious mind, visualizing excellence and being at one with himself. I helped him to build his confidence and give himself permission to be better than his father at something. The result was that, in the end, Tom broke the Guinness World Record with a drive over more than four-hundred-and-fifty yards. He went on to become the Senior PGA Long Drive Champion of North America. Tom thought it was I who cured him, but he cured himself with hypnosis. It was his victory, his triumph. He changed

Chapter 5 - It's All in Your Head   45

his brain and changed his game. Tom's father was elated by his son's success.

Creating Your Own Problems and Solutions

Another young man—I'll call him John—had the bad habit of "creating the impossible." He had a four handicap, so he was obviously an excellent golfer, but he had created for himself the reality that he couldn't make his short iron shots. When faced with a chip or short pitch, he'd say to himself, "Oh shit! I'm terrible at these shots. I can never hit a short iron cleanly. I just want to get this shot over with."

This was a story he told himself, not the truth, just a story. Now, as he approached his ball, the story he had constructed in advance of the facts, became a self-fulfilling prophecy. Mental events such as these produce toxic chemicals, which cause the muscles to tighten and all rhythm, timing and tempo to be lost. The result for John was just what his belief and expectation predicted and—Surprise! Surprise!—he *could not* make the short shot. The harder he tried, the worse he performed. He would inevitably top the ball or chunk it and end up playing army golf or chili dipping the hole.

Even his efforts at positive thinking yielded to the ironclad Law of Reverse Effect, so that saying, "I know I can do it," programmed his action mind *not* to do it and that is a painful conundrum. The other members of his regular foursome seemed to have contributed to this result as well. Since they gambled on each hole, whenever they saw John facing a chip shot, they would laugh hard and say, "This is where we start to leave you behind." Or they would say, "Show me the money!" Was there an element of gamesmanship in these comments or were they merely intended to state the historically predictability? Probably a little of both, but they clearly reinforced John's belief and expectation.

When John finally found his way to me, he was a very eager

client and proved easily hypnotizable. Along with equipping him with my standard self-hypnosis techniques for relaxation, concentration and visualization, I also designed special post-hypnotic suggestions specifically for him. Whenever John faced a short iron shot, he was to say to himself, "I used to freeze up on these shots. *I* choose not to do that anymore. I *now* have a fine touch for chips and pitches." This was really no more than a simple shifting of the words of John's story he told himself, and it had an immediate, immense impact. John called me the next day and said he had amazed his friends with his short iron shots. I was not surprised. I have seen similarly impressive results occur again and again, and all through no more than a subtle shift of your thoughts and your story. Let me say it again: "Change your brain—change your game."

Part 3:
The Game of the Spirit

Chapter 6:
And the Word Became Flesh

How can such small causes produce such large effects? The answer is belief and expectation. An example of something I see a lot here in my office is the story of two people, both of whom want to break into the movie business and become successful actors. One is a kid fresh off the bus from Iowa or wherever, who arrives in Hollywood and somehow lands an agent and a manager within a week or ten days. The other is a person who was born right here in the heart of the industry—she's trained, beautiful, talented—and she's tried and failed for years to get an agent to take her on or a manager to help make her a star. How can this be? How could someone with all the apparent advantages fail so consistently? How can fate be so unkind?

The answer, in a word, is *attitude*. Attitude is everything! The Los Angeles native says, "Oh boy, this town is tough. It is who you know. There is nothing here but snakes and sharks and users who smile in your face but cannot be trusted." The kid straight off the farm *does not know* that you cannot succeed overnight and so she *does* succeed overnight; while the native, who *knows* it's a tough racket to break into, makes that expectation become a reality. Your attitude makes it your truth. And is it *the* truth? No! It is just your story!

So the words of the gospel still ring true: "Whatsoever a man thinketh, so shall he be." You cannot get around what you think. If you *think* you are too old—for love, for sex, for golf—then you *are* too old. You *make* yourself too old. You make it your reality by thinking it so. If you think you are a lousy golfer, then you *are* a lousy golfer. Remember, *can't is a dirty, nasty four-letter word*. If you say, "I can't make this shot," then you *can't* make the shot. In a very real sense, to imagine is to create, and believing makes it so. This is as true in golf as it is in all of life's endeavors.

Iyanla Vanzant expresses this great life-truth with notable clarity and verve in her book *Until Today!* when she says, "We often say we want so many things while deep inside we doubt whether they will come to us. The universe does not give us what we say we want: it gives us what we expect to get. You cannot fool Mother Nature. She gives birth to your deepest thoughts and the principle is this: Everything happens twice, first on the inside, then on the outside. We must impregnate our total being with what we want. And believe it is so, then expect all the best right here and now."

Faith of this magnitude requires total commitment. As Vanzant concludes, "We must think about it, talk about it, expect it every moment, *and feel like we deserve it*." That last phrase is the big one. Once again, the bible says, "What so ever you pray for and believe that it is so, it will be so." The hard part is belief.

When you have a difficult lie on the golf course, take a moment, ask the golf gods, the universe, whatever you believe in, to be there to help you. And before you make your play, thank them. Of the great variety of negative, self-defeating thoughts and feelings I encounter in my practice, the one I see most frequently, is simply low self-esteem, the feeling that we're not really worthy of having joyful, successful, good things happen to us. We don't "feel like we deserve it." Why is this?

The core of our self-image lies within the deepest layers of our personality, but its effects can be seen every day. It is easy to pay attention only to things that are wrong, to be the critic who always finds fault. It's easy to find a reason to feel bad, to feel uncomfortable, and to hide from ourselves and others. And it's easy not to like ourselves or not to trust ourselves. All that is easy. It's much harder to summon the courage necessary to see things in a different light, to take risks and to enjoy ourselves, our lives and other people. Or is it?

Another emotion is fear. My sessions with golfers often reveal a paralyzing fear of failing or of looking foolish, even the fear of succeeding. We will turn to the fascinating subject of golf's emotions, and the ego-entanglements that breed them, but I first want to mention the greatest golf lesson that hypnosis teaches. I would like to tell you this general truth in the form of a story.

What's Getting in Your Way?

When I first began playing golf—I was *only* sixty-eight—I found that I couldn't manage to hit a drive more than about seventy-five to ninety yards. I just wasn't getting the distance I felt I was capable of, but I couldn't for the life of me figure out what the problem was.

One day I was at the driving range, working on my not-so-long ball, when the local pro came strolling by. I had seen him around the driving range before, but I'd never had a chance to speak with him. I could tell he was watching me as I began practicing my drives.

After a minute or so, he said to me, "Good morning. You know, I have seen you here before and you always have a beautiful smile."

I smiled and replied, "Why, thank you."

He smiled back and then said, "Do you mind if I make a small suggestion regarding your swing?"

I asked him laughingly, "Are you hustling me for lessons?" He assured me he was not. He said he had been watching me and that he could do one thing to improve my swing and get more distance.

I said, "Okay, what's that?"

He said, "I don't mean to be fresh, but it has to do with your breasts. They get in the way of your swing."

I was a little taken aback, as I am no Dolly Parton. But I must admit, he seemed so earnest and he was clearly intent on telling me something that would improve my drive.

He very quickly added, "Now please don't misunderstand me. I mean no disrespect, but I say this in all seriousness. Your breasts are getting in the way of your swing. Now, if you simply bring your arms a little more forward in front of your breasts and hold your elbows like so"—he modeled the posture—"then I think you will be able to put a lot more power into your drives as you will be able to follow through with your swing."

He was exactly right, of course. I immediately gained about thirty yards on most of my drives. But that wasn't all I gained. I also came away from that brief encounter with a concrete illustration of the primary lesson I seek to impart to my golfing clients: *Get out of your own way!* I insisted on giving him twenty dollars and wondered as he walked away, if I had just been hustled.

This idea sounds simple enough, if a little paradoxical, but as the many examples in this book show, it is your mental frames, your paradigms and your presuppositions that most often undermine your efforts toward improving your golf game (as well as your life). Far more than lifting your head, improperly rotating your hips, or any other mechanical errors, your mind is your own worst enemy. Your *thinking* mind, that is.

Imagine you are teeing off on the first hole. Everyone's watching, waiting. Your thinking mind says, "Oh God, I hope I don't hit a mulligan." Guess what? The fear in your thinking mind immediately becomes manifested in reality. What was a thought on the inside, happens on the outside. In other words, you

Chapter 6 - And the Word Became Flesh

hit a mulligan. You have to create the shot mentally before you do it physically. You have to be at one with the ball. You have to focus on where you want it to go. You have to believe in yourself and tell yourself that you do this all the time. You know how to hit a golf ball. Then, Wham! You swing with ease, grace and power.

As we have seen, thoughts affect us physically as well as mentally. I have shown you exactly how thoughts affect your physical self. Now you can see how simple it is to change your habits and thought patterns. As simple as one plus one is two. Most of us want to make it very complex. Remember, all of your learning takes place in the action mind, the sub-conscious part of your mind. Hypnosis allows the conscious mind to be lulled into a peaceful, relaxed state. It goes on a little vacation and the critical censor stops interfering. The thinking mind stops chattering with its endless "yeah buts" and "woulda-coulda-shouldas." Hypnosis is a powerful tool that you can use to help you get out of your own way.

Chapter 7:
Think Nothing. Feel Nothing. Be Nothing.

As we have seen, there are three stumbling blocks to the path of golfing excellence: the thinking mind, the emotions and the ego. These together do more than anything else to inhibit golf—or the art of living. It is that intense.

Fred Shoemaker's description of the average golfer's mindset that he carries to the first tee reveals these stumbling blocks, which we are going to turn into stepping stones. The average golfer is highly critical and judgmental toward other golfers and toward himself. This is the conscious mind at its most merciless, relentlessly calculating, evaluating and criticizing all things and all people.

The thinking mind dominates us, with thousands of little mechanical lessons and checklists of dos-and-don'ts and then muscular tension automatically follows. Beta waves fill the brain and the message sent to the action mind is often one of failure. In spite of this, most golfers constantly dwell on their body mechanics. You constantly think about your score. You play the whole course at once instead of one shot at a time, let alone one hole at a time. You get angry on the course and you turn to emotions—and once you are angry, your deep breathing stops, which in turn causes muscle tension to interfere with the physical mechanics. This is the rhythm and flow of your game. Before you know it, you are ready to throw your clubs in the lake.

When I lived in Hawaii, my condominium overlooked the eighteenth hole. Many evenings I would sit on my lanai, drink a Mai Tai and watch the golfers. If I did not know any swear words, I would have learned them there. I have seen golfers throw clubs, scream obscenities and even break very expensive clubs over

Chapter 7 - Think Nothing. Feel Nothing. Be Nothing.

their knees. One evening, I watched a golfer calmly walk over to his golf bag. He picked it up and dumped all of his clubs on the putting green. He then proceeded to throw all of them as far as he could. Then he got in the golf cart, with everyone from the condominium complex laughing at him, and drove away, leaving the clubs behind. An hour later he skulked back, sheepishly looking around, hoping that no one was watching him. He picked up each golf club and gently placed it in his bag. He then got back in his cart and drove away.

Even golf coaches, who know very little about hypnosis, have long been aware of the thinking mind's tendency to block success. The legendary English golf coach Percy Boomer once told his students, "You must be mindful but not thoughtful as you swing. You must not think or reflect." Excellent advice, but it's one thing to tell a golfer, "You must not think," and it's quite another to equip the golfer with the ability to silence the conscious mind, to literally think nothing. This can be achieved through the power of hypnosis.

When it comes to golf's emotions, we have Shoemaker's witty observation that every golfer is just two shots away from becoming a raving lunatic. I'm more inclined to think it's a one-shot gap for many of you. Slice your first drive out of bounds or skull your first fairway shot and you are apt to be muttering curses the rest of the round. This is always the way when emotion overpowers the thinking mind, which is already misdirecting the action mind. Emotions can literally carry us away. No matter how beautiful the day, no matter how great the spirit, a couple of bad shots in a row will bring out the vicious beast in many a golfer.

It is this general tendency of human beings that led Hamlet to say, "Give me that man that is not passion's slave, and I will wear him in my heart's core." That he likely died with an empty heart is a testament to the power of emotion. Percy Boomer was aware of this stumbling block too. Regarding the mind-body dynamics of the swing, he said, "You must *feel* what you have to do." These movements are controlled by muscle memory. Muscle memory is the well-trained body's own wisdom at work, the action of muscles that have learned to move correctly, spontaneously, by second nature. These bodily feelings, however, are far different from the feelings of anger and frustration that so often impede them.

Teed Off

Anger is the most destructive emotion on the golf course. It tenses the muscles and clouds the brain. When you're angry, your breathing is very shallow and you are not adequately oxygenating the brain and the muscles. It is worth remembering that the brain uses one-third of all the oxygen that the lungs take in, and the muscles, organs, nerves and tissues use the rest. When you are angry, it is impossible for you to play your best. You need tools to help you cool down. Consider this: Deepak Chopra says when he is hot, he imagines an icicle in his rectum. Well, that's certainly one way to cool down! If you don't have quite that powerful an imagination, then just *stop* and take your three deep breaths (see Appendix B). While inhaling, tell yourself that you are calm and relaxed. As you exhale, tell yourself that you are letting go of all stress and anger. Concentrate on your body and *feel* yourself relaxing. Do this three times, and you will be able to let go and swing easily and effortlessly.

Another element in Shoemaker's "package" is our strong desire to be admired as golfers, to look good by hitting a superb drive, to impress the gallery or our friends. Remember, we drive for show and we putt for dough!

I heard a wonderful story regarding ego. Jesus and Moses were playing golf. When they got to the seventh hole, Jesus took out a three iron.

Moses said, "J.C. this drive is impossible to make with a three iron!"

Chapter 7 - Think Nothing. Feel Nothing. Be Nothing.   55

J.C. replied, "I saw Arnold Palmer do it and so can I." Moses watched as J.C. placed the tee and hit the ball right into the water. Frustrated, J.C. looked at Moses and said, "Okay, part the water so I can get my ball!" Moses parted the water and J.C. got his ball. He cleaned it off, placed it back on the tee and took out his three iron. Once again, Moses reminded him that it was the wrong club for this hole. J.C. said, "If Arnold Palmer can do it, I can do it!" Once again he swung and—plop—right back in the water. "Okay," said J.C. "part the water again." Moses refused, so J.C. walked out on the water to retrieve his ball.

With that, the next foursome arrived and one of the men said, "Wow, would you look at that guy! Who does he think he is, Jesus Christ?"

And Moses replied, "No, he thinks he's Arnold Palmer!"

This is pure ego, of course, even for J.C. Now psychologically speaking, your ego is really no more than the conscious point of intersection between your thinking mind and action mind. Of course we mustn't tell the ego this, because it thinks it's really something, running the show and calling all the shots.

Looking good, the insatiable desire for approval and the deep-seated fear of criticism, is constraining for many of us. The impact of this creates a weak spot in our golf game. In Michael Murphy's wonderful little novel, *Golf in the Kingdom*, the character Shivas Irons gives Murphy some swing advice: "Let the nothingness into your shots," he says. Here, Murphy points to the final mystery of golf, that is, the mystery of being. Many religious and spiritual traditions show us that being and nothingness are in an intricately balanced dance.

M. Scott Peck points out this notion in his book *Golf and the Spirit*, when he speaks of a technique he calls *kenosis*, a practice in which "the self empties the self of the self." Now I know all you jocks are rolling your eyes, but before you close your mind altogether, consider a few facts. By using the positive techniques of hypnosis, you can easily attain what sport psychologists, coaches and athletes call being "in the zone," that feeling of being in the groove, where every move is perfect. This mental state allows you to center your attention and energies exclusively on the task at hand. In effect, you forget yourself when in the zone.

The Golfing Addiction

Each of these three stumbling blocks—thinking, feeling and ego—can be avoided with hypnosis. I want to discuss one of golf's most pleasantly ambivalent emotions: addiction. Is golf addictive? You bet it is. Players will play in the rain, wind, heat and the cold.

When I first started playing golf, I was not content with one bucket of balls. I had to get two or three. One day on the driving range, a handsome man around my age started hitting balls next to me. He caught my eye and smiled. I smiled back.

He said, "Can I tell you something?"

Inside, I groaned and thought, *Is this the sport where men are always giving you advice or telling you what to do?* Outside, I smiled and said, "Of course you can."

He looked at me, laughed and said, "Quit now! This game is like a drug and it is addictive."

He was right! But only if you love it. I took my daughter to the driving range, got her a bucket of balls and gave her a club. She hated it from her first swing. She has never tried it again and says it is the most hateful thing she has ever done. It just goes to show you, different strokes for different folks.

When I was playing golf on the island of Hawaii, it started to rain—a real tropical downpour. I was soaked in little more than a minute. My golf partner, a male friend of mine, asked if I wanted to quit. Now remember, at this time I was seventy-one. I said, "Hell no! How much wetter can we get?" And so we played on.

Chapter 7 - Think Nothing. Feel Nothing. Be Nothing.

I lost a lot of balls in the lava traps that round, but I had a glorious time. It's still one of my most vivid golfing memories. Everyone was sitting on their lanais, watching these two drenched idiots tee off in a tropical storm. I do not recommend that you play in a thunder storm. Lee Travino was hit by lightening twice on the golf course.

Once I played on a Thanksgiving morning when the wind was blowing so hard, I had to stand still and watch which way my pant legs were blowing to know how to hit my shot. The next day, I discovered that several huge trees had been blown down exactly where we had been playing.

On another occasion, in Southern California, my shot landed about six inches from the cup and out wandered a coyote from the brush, who walked over to sniff my ball. He was lean and mean. The three men in my foursome started laughing.

"Forget it," I said, "I'll just lose the ball."

"Oh, no you don't," they chimed in unison. "You have to play it as it lies."

What good sports! I decided that no matter what, I would not let them shame me. I walked right up to that coyote. He stood staring at me (I gave him the stink eye) for the better part of a minute, then he put his tail between his legs and took off. And to top it all off, I missed the six-inch putt. Is golf addictive or what?

One early morning my partner and I were playing golf when a car parked on the street (adjacent to the third hole) caught fire. Flames were shooting high in the air. We were ready to putt and I had a great lie. We putted with the heat of the flames at our backs. The car could have exploded, but at least I made my birdie. We ran very fast from the area, only after all of us had made our putts. The man who owned the car came running up and when he saw it was totally burned up, he turned around and went back to his game. He said as he walked away, "It can't burn any more. Burnt is burnt!"

So yes, golf is addictive. It seems you either love it or you hate it. Chasing a little white ball all over God's green earth for four hours at a stretch? Sounds more like "a good walk spoiled," as Mark Twain famously summarized his view of the sport. What could possibly be so alluring about it? Well, perhaps not much, but just wait until you hit one *really good shot* and feel a sense of satisfaction and accomplishment that is like no other. It's that one good shot that makes you forget the ninety-nine bad ones.

The truth is that a golf shot is neither good nor bad. It just is. It is what it is. The thinking mind's critical assessment of a shot is what attaches moral value to it, what makes it "good" or "bad." Still, these judgments are sometimes irresistible. Even so, enlightened golfer Deepak Chopra says, "Here, every once in a while, I can hit a ball like Tiger Woods, and that's good." Yes, golf is addictive.

The Cheaters

Chopra also says, cheating at golf is a source of bad karma! This brings me back to the three stumbling blocks. As an amateur golfer and a professional hypnotherapist, I discovered that I could discern what my fellow players' characters were by the way they behaved on the course.

There are people who fudge and cheat on their scores. Some are brazen. They will proudly announce a three-stroke hole when it was obvious to everyone else that they really shot a five—and never blink an eye. Others are shiftier. They'll say, "Well, now let's see. I hit one over there and another over there. I think it was a four." But you can be sure it was a six or seven. There are some who hit wimpy little shots and say, "Oh! That does not count." There are lots of lies—excuse the pun—on the golf course.

Cheating is bad for your golf game, because when we lie or cheat, we release toxic chemicals into the bloodstream. Every cell in our body reacts with tension when we lie or cheat. If you

Chapter 7 - Think Nothing. Feel Nothing. Be Nothing.

lie and cheat on the course, your swing becomes jerky instead of smooth and loose. If you aren't as good as your word, if you lack integrity, your body knows it, your brain knows it, and your golf game shows it.

Solving the Problems

Let me illustrate how hypnosis can cure three closely related and often inseparable behaviors in golf: choking, putting yips and first-tee jitters. Have you ever been in a clutch golf situation—approaching a six-inch putt on the eighteenth green? You found that your stroke had become wooden and unnatural and that you miss the easiest of shots. You know what it means to choke. It is your worst nightmare. Similarly, the yips are spasmodic movements of the hand or wrist that can affect even the best golfers. The yips mostly strike golfers when putting, but they can also affect other shots. The exact cause of the yips is unknown, although certain complex neurological conditions and performance anxiety are the usual suspects. Finally, first-tee jitters are so well known as to require no explanation. Performance anxiety is the root cause.

The yips and choking appear to be slightly different reactions to stress and anxiety. When choking occurs, the stroke becomes so rigid and mechanical that all fluidity and grace is lost. The player no longer trusts his muscle memory, but thinks through each position in the swing, rather than just trusting the swing. The yips, on the other hand, crop up when anxiety and fear create a sense of panic. You freeze up and cannot think or even act without difficulty. Both are related to stress and anxiety, but that is where the similarity ends.

The yips occur commonly during putts shorter than five feet, less frequently during tee and iron shots. Studies show, when playing the same putts, golfers who have the yips have anxiety levels similar to golfers who don't have the yips. Those who experience the yips appear to have a faster heart rate and increased muscle activity in the wrists. They tend to grip the putter with greater force. Golfers with the yips process far more activity in the left brain than the right brain. Putters who use both sides of the brain equally, tend to putt better.

As you have been reading this book, you can easily see the solutions for the yips, choking and the jitters, using the three-breath exercise in Appendix B. I also suggest using your own personal post-hypnotic suggestion in the Golf Script (see Appendix D). Here are a few ideas: "My putting is smooth and fluid. My wrists are loose and flexible. My forearm muscles and wrist muscles are relaxed and graceful. I see where my putt will go. It is where I have chosen to send it. My stroke is smooth as silk. I am confident, capable and relaxed."

A powerful, embedded, post-hypnotic suggestion is even more effective than the administration of drugs called beta-blockers. We know from experience that hypnosis will achieve relaxation under stressful situations. Hypnosis can relieve your anxiety, improve your concentration, empower visualization and help you successfully overcome emotional traps, such as the fear of failure, fear of success and even your fear of ridicule.

Chapter 8:
Let Go. Let Golf.

There's power in numbers, in sports as in life. Individual sports generally require more spirit than do team sports, where enthusiasm is contagious. The spirit of the solitary golfer must come from within. The loneliness of the long-distance runner applies equally well to golfers.

You alone carry the full responsibility for success. There are no excuses in golf. The thrill of victory is yours alone. You alone feel the pressure. In golf, there is no one trying to return your serve or pin you to a mat or checkmate you. It's just you against the golf course. Tournaments are competitive events and sometimes the friendliest Sunday foursomes can be even more competitive.

You can see that when it comes to golf, the spirit of the game is in fact the game of the spirit. All you hardened left-brainers may roll your eyes at this last claim. Before your scoffing closes your ears entirely, I ask, Why is it that golf, of all sports, has inspired the most varied metaphysical speculations? Every sport has its philosophies, but they are often little more than anecdotes. No, golf is different. The nature of the game is its spaciousness, its pace, its very triviality, which fosters a transcendental attitude in players. Golf seems to bring us close to the mystical heart of things.

The Agony and the Ecstasy

Agon is a Greek word that seems remarkably relevant to some of our most common golfing emotions. We *agonize* over our drives, our pitches, our chips and our putts, and some rounds of golf are sheer *agony*. The core meaning of *agon* was not pain, however, but *struggle*. *Agon* was used to describe struggles of all kinds, from athletic competitions to dramatic festivals to contentions in law courts. *Ecstasy* is another Greek word. In modern English we use it to describe a state of maximum pleasure, satisfaction, bliss and joy. This word is seldom applied to the game of golf. Great satisfactions are few, even for the most accomplished players. Golf's satisfactions are most often mixed with anxious anticipation of future hazards, the sand trap, the water and the rough. Ecstasy in its original sense meant something quite different from what it means today. For the Greeks it meant to be standing or dwelling outside yourself. If you're standing outside yourself, it allows the god, the breath of the spirit, to seize your body as a channel of divine influence. In golf, we find ourselves by losing ourselves. The agony is the ecstasy. By letting go of our ego, by being, we find harmony.

Golf should be an exercise of perfect freedom. Just what does this mean? It means when you step up to take your shot, and your mind is filled with formulas, checklists or swing mechanics, you are not free. If looking good and not being embarrassed are important to you, you are not free. If you are fearful or hopeful, you are not free. Did you know children are the best putters? They do not think, they have no fear, they just do it. Now that is freedom.

Freedom is knowing that it *is all* up to you. I repeat, "Whatsoever you pray for and believe that it is so, it *will* be so." This is the innermost secret of hypnosis. Deepak Chopra has made a similar point in describing how thoughts create realities by means of mechanisms that operate at the level of quantum physics. Remember, a thought is not just an idle thing flitting through your mind. Science now understands that a thought becomes a molecule, a measurable energy unit. These molecules become messengers in a nanosecond, going to every cell in your body. As you think a thought, you are involved in mind and body connections. In reality, you are a body and thoughts. Your thoughts create your behavior. If you want to change your behavior on the golf course or anywhere else in your life, change your thoughts and the behavior will change almost automatically. This will bring about a change in your game and your life.

Chopra talks of focusing your attention on an idea; don't define it, don't analyze it, don't interpret it. Just have your intention on your goal and that will cause a change, a positive transformation in your consciousness and your life. What he says applies to golf. By concentrating and visualizing, we turn out thoughts into truths, the truths of reality. According to Hindu and Buddhist teachings, thoughts can make it so. On the golf course, these are grounds for confident beliefs and great expectations.

Golf Course 101

Golf is a beautiful sport. It opens a window into our souls. Our egos might wish to hear nothing but praise and be assured that we are gods, but we are not here on this planet because we are perfect beings. No, we are here because we have work to do. We have lessons to learn when we play the game of golf and the game of life.

I say this to many of my clients who have problems with anger. Golf shows us what we need to work on, both in our golf game and in our life. Many of my clients have problems with anger. Many golfers are acutely aware of their anger when they play golf. Simple mistakes can lead to fits of screaming and swearing. A shot hooked out of bounds results in someone breaking his expensive driver over his knee. A ball landing in a sand trap or water hazard is cause for blowing up. He could fix that hook by learning to keep the swing plane level, but do you think that would solve his rage problem? No, his rage would simply emerge somewhere else, when his chipping game had problems or after he missed a crucial putt.

Golf teaches us who we are, where to seek improvement and how to nurture our souls. I know many golfers who are good in one or two aspects of the game. Perhaps they can drive the ball very well or putt superbly, but their game is not complete. They're weak in some aspect of their game. What golf might be teaching them is that they may be incomplete and fragmentary in their life. Golf teaches them that they're impatient. They find themselves always rushing, not taking the time to do their practice swings or to properly read the green before putting. Others realize that they cannot play it straight. They lie and cheat to suit their needs. Still others are defeated when they are under the slightest pressure.

Why don't they use these opportunities to find out where they fall short and what their spirit needs to learn in life?

Hypnosis can be used to work on these problems just as easily as it can be used for weight loss, to stop smoking or a myriad of other problems. Golf hypnosis can improve your life as well as your game. Now perhaps you are thinking to yourself, *This is too much. I am such a pathetic, miserable failure that I will never get it right. I never will overcome my rages or learn to be a whole person.* Do not despair. That's not the truth. It is just a story that you are telling yourself.

I am going to let you in on a well-known secret that might cheer you up: You can do it. It will take some courage, some determination and the willingness to pick yourself up after you fall. You have the courage to do something about it now if you really put your mind to it!

Remember, you have to go out on the limb to get the sweetest fruit. You can cling to the trunk and play it safe or you can let go and climb out on the limb. Go for it and get that sweetest fruit. What if the limb breaks? Well, you can pick yourself up, dust yourself off and start all over again. One "bad" shot on the golf course is not the whole game, just as one mistake in any endeavor is not the end.

Chapter 8 - Let Go. Let Golf. 65

I would like to share parts of my two favorite Sufi poems. They pertain to your going for it, whether you're playing the game of golf or the game of life.

The master and the student were standing on a precipice. The master said to the student, "Come to the edge of the cliff." The student replied, "I can't, master. I am afraid." The master repeated himself, "Come to the edge of the cliff," and once again the student said, "I can't. I am afraid." This time, the master commanded the student, "Come to the edge of the cliff now." The student came to the edge of the cliff with great trepidation. When the student reached the edge, the master shoved him *and he flew!*

The second is this: The pebble had to break away from the boulder in order to become a grain of sand, in order to be washed out to sea, in order to get under the oysters shell, in order to become a pearl.

Do not be afraid to go to the edge or break away when you are playing golf. That is what is needed to improve your game. Your attitude will make a difference. Take the chance. Why not go out on a limb? Why not go to the edge of the cliff? Why not break away from the boulder? Dare to make the most of yourself. Really use the powers of self-hypnosis to tackle the issues that have been haunting you. Think about it. Here you are, reading a book telling you to deal with your issues. What an incredible occurrence! From the very first moments of the universe, this moment was preparing itself, waiting to happen and now it is here. Now the time has come when your truth is being offered to you. What are you going to do?

Golf is a blessed game. It shows you the very state of your soul. If you have hitches in your game, then you have hitches in your soul. Your soul has been around for a long time. The problems you are having with your golf game very likely point to problems that your soul has been wrestling with for as long as you can imagine. Be courageous. Be brave. Dare to take on these problems directly. Dare to challenge these issues. Heck, you might even knock a few strokes off your game.

Go for it!

Appendix A: Doing The Dirty Work

Remember at the beginning of this book I told you that you would be doing the "dirty work?" Well, now it is time. You are going to eliminate your stumbling blocks and turn them into stepping stones. You are going to begin to make positive suggestions to your sub-conscious mind, your action mind. The part that acts on the suggestions, thoughts and instructions you give it.

However, just affirming over and over again that you are a great golfer, that you putt with poise and skill will not quite get you there, because your conscious mind has the critical censor that interferes and says, "Oh yeah?" "Sure?" "Who are you kidding?" While these suggestions will take hold over a long period of time, that's not good enough. We live in a time of instant gratification. When something does not happen quickly, we just give up. The other issue is that while the sub-conscious mind is so powerful, it is also very particular about how you talk to it! You cannot just tell it that you want to improve your golf game. That is too vague. Who, what, where, when and why are the things that need to be addressed. For example:
(Please insert your name in the blanks.)

I, _____, am going to lower my 100 golf score by 10 points and consistently shoot in the 90s.

I, _____, choose to control my temper regardless of how poor a putt or drive I have made.

I, _____, will always be present (in the moment) and play one shot, one hole at a time.

I,_____, will always play my best, regardless of the circumstances.

I,_____, enjoy playing golf no matter what my score may be.

I,_____, focus on playing my best from the moment I tee off on the first hole.

You can see by these few examples that you must give your sub-conscious mind complete and direct suggestions. You cannot just say, "I want to play better." What does that mean? To the sub-conscious mind, nothing!

You are going to be sending your sub-conscious mind powerful suggestions. Be clear and specific. Always write down your wishes, wants and desires pertaining to your game of golf, and yes, your game of life. Then watch the miracles happen!

As you begin visualizing, the visualization will become the action. The visualization improves your muscle coordination. Have you ever competed against a particular opponent and felt yourself getting nervous and stressed out? Remember how you tightened up and played so poorly? This is an emotional problem. It has no bearing on your ability to play the game of golf. This is when you need your cue (the one you have chosen) and you need to focus, breathe, steady yourself, shut out all outside stimuli and open yourself to allow the muscle memory of your swing or putt to take over. Remember, your mental attitude will enable you to let go of the pressure, stress, anxiety, panic and ultimately ego.

Hypnosis is the tool that will help you eliminate the negative habits that interfere with your game. It will enable you to gain control, no matter what the circumstances. Always focus on how you want to perform. Know that your sub-conscious mind memorizes both good and bad performances. It does not know fantasy from reality. It makes no decisions, no judgments. It just does what you program it to do. Why not continually program confidence, success and a wonderful self-projection?

The hypnosis induction and Golf Script in Appendices C and D will help you re-program your sub-conscious mind. It will encourage you to let go of bad habits and incorporate new and empowering habits. Think about it, feel it and see it in your imagination while under hypnosis. This will help you reinforce the positive and eliminate the negative.

Trust your cue, trust your sub-conscious, trust your visualizations. Enhance the positive, rather than focusing on the negative. You will look forward to every day you play golf. You can become the golfer of your own choosing and that is going to feel wonderful.

More Dirty Work

Take your time filling out the following pages. Your answers will give you insights into yourself and your golf game. You will learn what you like about yourself and what you may choose to change. It is important that you do some self-evaluation. It is also important that you write down your deepest thoughts pertaining to the following questions. The answers are just for you, but the nice thing is you can go back and check what you have written and see the progress and changes you have made.

It is all about you!

Consider the following questions and write your answers in the spaces provided. Be as specific and honest as possible.

How do you feel when you are competing against your toughest opponent?

Do you feel insecure?

Do you feel self-defeated?

Do you feel frustrated?

Do you feel not good enough?

_____
_____
_____
_____
_____
_____
_____
_____
_____
_____
_____
_____
_____
_____

Appendix A

What do you do to release stress and tensions on the golf course?

Do you laugh?

Do you pout?

Do you breathe?

Do you get sarcastic?

Do you get nasty with the people you play with?

_____

_____

_____

_____

_____

_____

_____

_____

_____

_____

_____

_____

_____

_____

If you are gambling on each hole, do you win with dignity?

Lose with dignity?

Do you pay up at the end of the game?

Do you fudge and not pay?

Do you cheat if you are losing?

Appendix A

If you are competing, how do you feel?

Nervous?

Tense?

Exhilarated?

Excited?

_____
_____
_____
_____
_____
_____
_____
_____
_____
_____
_____
_____
_____
_____
_____
_____

If you are winning, do you…

Freeze up?

Feel enthralled?

Count your money?

Blow easy shots?

_____
_____
_____
_____
_____
_____
_____
_____
_____
_____
_____
_____
_____
_____
_____
_____
_____

If the gallery is watching your every move, do you…

Stay focused?

Breathe deeply?

Enjoy the attention?

Are you superstitious?

Do you always wear a specific color?

Do you always wear the same clothes?

Do you always play with certain clubs?

Are you afraid to change?

___

Appendix A

What is your goal regarding your golf game? Would you like to improve your:

Putting?

Drive?

Control of your emotions?

Enjoyment of the game?

_____

_____

_____

_____

_____

_____

_____

_____

_____

_____

_____

_____

_____

_____

What behaviors or habits do you need to change in order to reach your goal?

Appendix A

Visualize how you will feel when you achieve your goal:

Awesome?

Rewarded?

Relieved?

Inspired?

Triumphant?

_____
_____
_____
_____
_____
_____
_____
_____
_____
_____
_____
_____
_____
_____

How do people respond to you as your game improves?

Surprised?

Jealous?

Envious?

Complimentary?

_____
_____
_____
_____
_____
_____
_____
_____
_____
_____
_____
_____
_____
_____
_____
_____
_____

Now take your time and visualize your perfect game. Describe it in detail. Include the time of day, the course, the weather. Who are you with? Feel it. Sense it.

_____
_____
_____
_____
_____
_____
_____
_____
_____
_____
_____
_____
_____
_____
_____
_____
_____
_____
_____
_____
_____
_____

What changes did you implement to achieve your perfect game?

Did you let go of anger?

Did you stop criticizing yourself?

Did you let go of shame? Of the need to look good?

Did you let go of ego?

_____
_____
_____
_____
_____
_____
_____
_____
_____
_____
_____
_____
_____
_____
_____
_____

Appendix A

How did you handle yourself after your best game?

Did you show off?

Were you arrogant?

Did you drink? Did you have a joint?

Did you brag?

Did you feel proud?

Did you analyze?

Were you grateful?

_____
_____
_____
_____
_____
_____
_____
_____
_____
_____
_____
_____

For Golfers and Other Athletes

What steps did you take to maximize your enjoyment of the game?

Did you play one hole at a time?

Did you enjoy your surroundings?

Did you feel alive?

Did you let go and just play the game?

Appendix A

How will you handle an occasional set back?

Will you get pressured?

Will you break a club?

Will you tear up your score card?

Will you tear up?

Will you try to do better next time?

_____
_____
_____
_____
_____
_____
_____
_____
_____
_____
_____
_____
_____
_____
_____

What cue have you chosen to gain control of yourself and on the golf course?

Please choose one now.

Make it a powerful one for you.

___
___
___
___
___
___
___
___
___
___
___
___
___
___
___
___
___

Appendix B:
Breathing: The Breath of Life

Throughout this book, I have mentioned taking deep, oxygenating, relaxing breaths. Now, of course we are all breathing or we would be dead! I am talking about purposeful breathing, focusing on your breathing, stretching out you lungs and then exhaling very slowly. I am not talking about sucking in your belly, sticking out your chest and then exhaling a great gulp of air. Breathing this way will make you hyperventilate. We certainly do not want that to happen on the golf course or anywhere else. As much as I am against smoking, especially on the driving range or on the golf course, observe the way people inhale on a cigarette. They take a deep drag, hold that smoke in their lungs and then they exhale very slowly. They then erroneously give the cigarette credit for relaxing them. It is not the cigarette, it is their deep breathing. Of course, after many years of smoking, they will not be able to take a deep breath.

You are going to begin practicing deep breathing, at least three deep breaths, five times a day, in the car, at a board meeting, watching TV, in heavy traffic and on the golf course. Remember Rudyard Kipling's poem "If"? The first stanza is, "If you can keep your head when all about you/ Are losing theirs and blaming it on you,/ Yours is the Earth and everything that's in it,/ And—which is more—you'll be a Man, my son!" You can achieve this total control by purposeful breathing. As you take your deep breath, let your stomach stick out, then hold it. Open your mouth slightly and exhale as slowly as you can. Feel how good it feels, so practice, practice, practice.

As you inhale, silently tell your self, "I am relaxing." As you exhale, tell yourself "Letting go of stress and tension." After a while, you will only have to do only one deep breath in any stressful situation, because you will have programmed your sub-conscious mind to recognize that a deep breath is a signal to relax. Imagine how you can help your golf game after a disastrous shot. Breathe as though your golf game depends on it. Practice, practice, practice.

Appendix C:
Your Induction

An induction is used to put you into an hypnotic state. All inductions begin with three deep breaths (see Appendix B). The purpose of the induction is to relax you and to narrow your focus. It is important that you understand that you will be listening to the tape you make (or that you purchased from me) at night when you are ready to go to sleep. NEVER LISTEN WHILE YOU ARE DRIVING A CAR OR USING MACHINERY. You will be listening to your tape every night for twenty-one nights. Pavlov, the great Russian scientist, taught us that to change a dominate thought to a recessive thought takes twenty-one days. The damnable part is that the negative recessive thought is always there. We need to be the guardians of our thoughts. I remind you, you are what you think. Pay attention to what you say, what you do and what you think. The thoughts create who you are.

When you are making a tape or CD for yourself, remember this is not a drama, it is not an acting class. You want to read the induction in a monotonous voice, like a lullaby. Slowly, giving yourself time to do what is instructed. For example, "You are walking along the beach." Give yourself time to pick out your favorite beach, be there, sense it and feel it.

Leave space between each suggestion so you can implement them. The dots in the induction indicate where you should pause. Certain words are very hypnotic and you will draw those words out. Words such as smooooooth, or baaack and fooorth. These words are emphasized and said very slowly. Your induction should last about twenty minutes. Remember to leave yourself time to sense and feel and visualize the suggestions.

When you have completed your induction, you will then go to your Golf Script (Appendix D).

Again, always begin with three deep breaths before the induction. When you have finished the induction, go to the Golf Script. Listen to your tape or CD every night, allowing yourself to fall asleep knowing that your sub-conscious mind is always listening. Your sub-conscious mind has a hidden observer, always alert, always listening. Have you ever had a chiming clock? The first ten days you hear it every hour on the hour. After a while you no longer hear it… consciously, but your sub-conscious mind is still listening and somehow knows that it is just a clock, nothing to worry about.

Induction

Close your eyes…
Make yourself very comfortable.
Take your time…
That's right… (pause)
Take a deep breath…
through your nose…
Inhaling…
Filling your lungs until you cannot get any more air in…
Hooooold it…
Open your mouth slightly…
Aaaaand exhale veeeery slowly…
The more slowly you exhale, the more your body will relax… unwind… slow down…
Good… (said very softly)
(longer pause)
Inhaling once again...
Deeeeeep breath…
Fill your lungs until you can't get any more air in…
Hold it…

Appendix C

Focus on your breathing...
Open your mouth slightly...and
Exhale veeeery slowly...
Feeeeel how good it feels... To just empty your lungs and relax... unwind... and let go...
That's right...(said softly)
(longer pause)
Inhaling once again...
A deep gentle breath...
Filling your lungs... stretching them out...
Hold-it...
Open your mouth slightly...
And exhale veeeery slowly and as you exhale feel your body relaxing... From the top of your head... Down to the tips of your toes... Good... (said softly)
Continue to focus on your breathing... Breathing easily and effortlessly and comfortably...
Inhaling relaxation...
Exhaling all stress and tension...
In just a few moments you are going to be more relaxed than you have even been before...
(slight pause)
In order to help you relax...
I want you to visualize yourself on a beautiful golf course...
You are alone... and safe...
No one and nothing can harm you...
It is your favorite golf course....
(longer pause)
You find yourself...walking along the beautiful, green course...
You are barefoot
Feeeeel the warm... soft... smooth grass beneath your feet...
The warm sun relaxing every muscle...
every fiber of your being...

Inhale the fragrant fresh air...
Feeeeel the soft, gentle breeze on your body...
You find yourself walking along a small, tree-lined lake...
The lake is surrounded with colorful...fragrant flowers...
you walk slowly down to the water's edge...
The soft breeze is gently swaying the trees...
And forming small, gentle waves along the shore of the lake...
You step into the cool, refreshing water...
It swirls around your feet and ankles...
Aaaand you stand relaxed... at ease... letting go...
Watching the gentle waves form... And roll in... and out...
In... and... out...
(said very slow)
relaxed...
letting go...
slowing down...
(long pause)
You turn and walk along the water's edge among the trees... and the flowers...
Listen... you can hear the birds singing in the trees...
Under the shade of a tree is a soft and comfortable rocking chair...
You stroll over to the chair and sit down...
Make yourself *sooooo* comfortable...
As your chair begins to gently rock you...Baaaack and fooooorth...Baaaack and fooooorth... Relax... letting go... Slowing down...
(longer pause)
Now in just a moment...
In order to help you relax even more...
I'm going to mention certain parts of your body...
As I mention *each* part of your body just let that part relax...
Starting with your forehead...

Appendix C

Feeeeel all the muscles in your forehead smooooooth out...
Feeeeeel all tension... leave...
And the relaxation moves down into your temple area now...
All around your eyes and all those muscles relax...
As those muscles relax...
Your eyelids feeeeel... sooooooo... heavy...
Your eyelids feel *so heavy*, so relaxed...
So tightly closed...
It *feels* as if you can barely open them...
And that's just fine...
You may feel your eyes moving around behind your eyelids...
And that's just fine...
Feeeeeel the relaxation move down into the facial area now...
And all the muscles in the facial area relax...
Feeeeeel your tongue relax in your mouth and your teeth part just a little...
Goooood...(said in whisper)
Now your mouth may open slightly as all the muscles in the face and jaw relax...
So much tension gathers in the jaw area...
But now you feel all the muscles in your jaw relax... and... *All tension leaves...*
(longer pause)
Feeeeeeel the relaxation moving up behind your ears now...
Down the back of your neck...
Deep into your shoulders...
And all *those* muscles... are now... loose... and... limp... Loose... and... limp...
(longer pause)
Feeeeeel the relaxation moving down your back now...
Down... down... down... your back...
Mooooooving down around the curve of your buttocks...
Down the back of your thighs...

Deeeeeep into the hollows of your knees...
Down the calves of your legs...
Around your ankles...
Deep into your heels...
And mooooving slowly... Into the soles of your feet...
As you go deeper and deeper and even deeper More and more relaxed...
It *feels* so good to relax, to unwind to let go...
(longer pause)
Feeeeel the relaxation moving deep into your throat now...
And all the muscles in your throat relax...
And the relaxation mooooves over the front of your shoulders...
Down your arms... around your wrists... Deep into your hands...
And down into each and every finger...
As you go deeper... and deeper... and even deeper...
You may feel tingling in your fingertips... And that's just fine....
You may feel warmth in the palms of your hands... And that's just fine...
your arms and your hands are so *heavy*...so *heavy*... so *heavy*...
Your arms and your hands... So *heavy*... so... relaxed... So comfortable that you can barely lift them...
And that's just fine...
(longer pause)
Now feeeeel the relaxation moving deep into the chest area...
And all the muscles and organs in the chest area relax...
And the warm, soothing sensation of relaxation...
Mooooves slowly into the abdominal area...
And the pelvic area...
And all those muscles and organs relax...
Feeeeel the relaxation moving over the tops of the thighs...
Down the shins, deep into the knees...
Around the ankles...
Deep into the insteps of the feet...

Appendix C

And down into each and every toe...
As you go deeper... and deeper... and even deeper...
More and more relaxed...
It feels so good... To relax... unwind... let go...
As you rock in your chair... Baaaack and foooorth... Baaaack and foooorth...
Feeling... the warmth of the sun on your body...
Inhaling the fragrant, healthy fresh air...
Listening to the soothing sound of my voice...
Allowing it to take you deeper... deeper... and even deeper...
Feeeeel the quietness filling your mind and your body...
(longer pause)
All right now... Doing very well...
In just a moment, I'm going to begin counting from seven to zero and as I count from seven to zero, and perhaps you would be willing, with each number I count, to go deeper and deeper, more and more relaxed...
and you will do this *not* because you *have* to, but because you really *want* to.
(longer pause)
Seven... deeper and deeper... six... five... even deeper... four... threeeee...down... down... down... twoooo... oooone... zeeeerooo... (At each number, lower and soften your voice, stretching out each number until you get to zero, which will be almost a whisper.)
Feeeeel the quietness... Fill your mind and your body and be still... be still... be still... (almost a whisper)
(longer pause)
(very intimate and softly) Sooooo... relaxed... Soooo... at ease... Soooo...comfortable... Your body relaxed...
Your conscious mind at ease...
Your conscious mind can listen or not listen...
Your conscious mind can think its own thoughts...

Your conscious mind can choose to forget...
To remember...
or remember to forget...
Whatever your conscious mind chooses to do will be just right for you...
I'm going to be working with your sub-conscious mind...
I'm going to be working with that part of your sub-conscious mind that is willing to be a...
relaxed... confident... golfer...a winner.
(Now proceed to the Golf Script in Appendix D.)

Appendix D: Golf Script

After your induction, you will record your Golf Script. Here, you should be more *assertive*, *positive* and *confident*. This is where we put the hypnotic suggestions into your sub-conscious mind that will enhance your golf game and eradicate any negativity connected with your game. This negativity is like a stumbling block that interferes with you perfecting your game. This script is a generic script and remember, different strokes for different folks. I do not use generic scripts in my office. Generic scripts are very helpful, however, I prefer to tailor scripts in a more personal way if someone comes to my office or works with me on the phone. When you have finished your Golf Script, you will have your tape or CD to listen to. You will listen to it every night for twenty-one nights. You will fall asleep and you will sleep well. You will improve your golf game.

For information on how to order your complete set of tapes or CDs, please see the back of this book.

I Love This Game

(To be used after the induction in Appendix C.)
Imagine yourself on your favorite golf course…take your time…
It is a beautiful day… You are relaxed… confident…
In your mind's eye… imagine yourself preparing to tee off…
You are waiting for your turn…
As you wait tell your self, I am relaxed…
Breathe... relax... let go of all tension…
Feel your muscles loose and limp... loose and limp…
Now place your ball on your tee…
Stand up… slowly…

Take a deep breath…
Breathe out all stress and tension…
Relax…
(act on your cue here, whatever you have chosen)
Focus on your target…
Take your time…nothing to worry about…
Take your practice swing…
Feel how loose and relaxed your swing is…
Focus on where you want your ball to… go…
See only the fairway…
Picture your ball landing on the fairway…
See and sense your ball landing… exactly where you want it to land…
You feel positive…
You feel very relaxed…
You feel very focused…
You are having a good time…
Now you step into your shot…
Swing your club back smoothly… slowly… naturally…
Trust your swing…
Let go of the mechanics…
Focus on the target…
Your grip is loose and natural…
All tension is gone…
Visualize the ball's flight…
Your body and mind know the set-up…
Your body and mind know how to get the ball to the target…
Shut off all thoughts…
Be unaware of all surroundings…
Just you and the ball and the target…
You… the ball… and the target…
Trust yourself that you will play well…
Focus on the positive…

Appendix D

Allow yourself the pleasure to play well...
Focus only on the target... nothing else...
Shut out all the hazards...
Shut out all outside stimuli...
Breathe... take your time... relax... and....
Let go and swing...
Tell yourself, "I am relaxed..."
Tell yourself, "I am having a good time..."
Tell yourself, "I will play the best I can..."
Tell yourself, "I have confidence in my ability..."
"I have the ability to concentrate..."
"I have the ability to focus on the target..."
Tell yourself, "I have the ability to follow through on my swing... I do this easily... effortlessly..."
Tell yourself, "Whether I am driving, chipping or putting, I am relaxed...
"I am in control..."
"I am focused..."
"I am confident... and I am having fun..."
And... watch the magic begin to happen.

(Pause for sixty seconds and then record the rest of the script...)

If you are going to sleep... you will fall into a deep and restful and peaceful sleep... Your sub-conscious mind will remain alert and listening...
recording every word on this tape deep into your sub-conscious mind... for you to draw on each and every day... to enable you to become the best golfer you can... and when you awaken in the morning... you will be rested... refreshed... and ready for a new day.... Before you even open your eyes... tell yourself... "I am a winner... I love playing golf... I am confident and always play the best I can... and that feels wonderful..."

If you are going to sleep you will sleep now. (Said very slowly and softly) Sleep...sleep...sleep...now...
No need to pay attention to the rest of the tape...

OR

(If you should be listening to this in the daytime and you need to come back up, wait sixty seconds and tell yourself a little more briskly...)

I am going to begin counting from one to three... as I count from one to three I will bring myself back up... I am going to feel very confident about my newfound ability to play golf... One coming up... feeling very, very good... Two coming up even more... Three, eyes wide open and feeling wonderful.

Appendix E:
Follow Your Bliss

Track your improvement. The following charts will help you see yourself improving your game. Be scrupulous! The charts give you permission to honestly track your game each time you play.

Enjoy seeing how you improve. Never get down when you have a bad day that is less than perfect for you. If you focus on the feeling of joy and freedom when you play, when you are on the golf course, you will discover that you are playing better. Celebrate a great drive. Be thrilled with a fantastic putt. Ignore the not-so-great drive or putt. Remember, there is always another day!

Hole	Yards	Par	HCP	Score	Notes
1					
2					
3					
4					
5					
6					
7					
8					
9					
10					
11					
12					
13					
14					
15					
16					
17					
18					
Totals					

Appendix E

Hole	Yards	Par	HCP	Score	Notes
1					
2					
3					
4					
5					
6					
7					
8					
9					
10					
11					
12					
13					
14					
15					
16					
17					
18					
Totals					

Hole	Yards	Par	HCP	Score	Notes
1					
2					
3					
4					
5					
6					
7					
8					
9					
10					
11					
12					
13					
14					
15					
16					
17					
18					
Totals					

Appendix E

Hole	Yards	Par	HCP	Score	Notes
1					
2					
3					
4					
5					
6					
7					
8					
9					
10					
11					
12					
13					
14					
15					
16					
17					
18					
Totals					

Hole	Yards	Par	HCP	Score	Notes
1					
2					
3					
4					
5					
6					
7					
8					
9					
10					
11					
12					
13					
14					
15					
16					
17					
18					
Totals					

Appendix E

Hole	Yards	Par	HCP	Score	Notes
1					
2					
3					
4					
5					
6					
7					
8					
9					
10					
11					
12					
13					
14					
15					
16					
17					
18					
Totals					

Hole	Yards	Par	HCP	Score	Notes
1					
2					
3					
4					
5					
6					
7					
8					
9					
10					
11					
12					
13					
14					
15					
16					
17					
18					
Totals					

Appendix E

Hole	Yards	Par	HCP	Score	Notes
1					
2					
3					
4					
5					
6					
7					
8					
9					
10					
11					
12					
13					
14					
15					
16					
17					
18					
Totals					

Hole	Yards	Par	HCP	Score	Notes
1					
2					
3					
4					
5					
6					
7					
8					
9					
10					
11					
12					
13					
14					
15					
16					
17					
18					
Totals					

Hole	Yards	Par	HCP	Score	Notes
1					
2					
3					
4					
5					
6					
7					
8					
9					
10					
11					
12					
13					
14					
15					
16					
17					
18					
Totals					

Bibliography: Golf

Chopra, Deepak. *Golf for Enlightenment: The Seven Lessons for the Game of Life*. New York: New Harmony, 2003.

Cohn, Patrick J. *The Mental Game of Golf*. Lantham, Md.: Taylor, 1994.

Coop, Richard with Bill Fields. *Mind Over Golf*. New York: Wiley, 1993.

Gallwey, W. Timothy. *The Inner Game of Golf*. New York: Random House, 1998.

Graham, D. *Mental Toughness Training for Golf*. New York: Stephen Green-Pellham, 1990.

Hendricks, Gay. *Conscious Golf: The Three Secrets of Success in Business, Life and Golf*. New York: Rodale, 2003.

Huff, Byron. *Be the Target: How to Let Go and Play the Game of Golf*. Chicago: Contemporary Books, 1996.

Jones, Charlie and Kim Doren. *Be the Ball: A Golf Instruction Book for the Mind*. Kansas City: Stark, 2000.

McCord, Gary. *Golf for Dummies: A Reference for the Rest of Us*. 2nd ed. New York: Wiley, 1999.

Murphy, Michael. *Golf in the Kingdom*. New York: Viking, 1972.

Murphy, Michael. *The Kingdom of Shivas Irons*. New York: Broadway Books, 1999.

Murphy, Michael and Rhea A. White. *The Psychic Side of Sports*. Reading, Mass.: Addison, 1978.

Parent, Joseph. *Zen Golf: Mastering the Mental Game*. New York: Doubleday, 2002.

Peck, M. Scott. *Golf and the Spirit: Lessons for the Journey*. New York: Three Rivers, 1999.

Reilly, Rick. *Who's Your Caddy?: Looping for the Great, Near Great and Reprobates of Golf*. New York: Broadway, 2003.

Rotella, Bob and Bob Cullen. *The Golfer's Mind: Play to Play Great*. New York: Free Press, 2004.

Shoemaker, Fred and Peter Shoemaker. *Extraordinary Golf: The Art of the Possible*. New York: Perigee, 1996.

Winters, Robert K. *The Ten Commandments of Mindpower Golf: No-Nonsense Strategies for Mastering Your Mental Game*. New York: McGraw, 2004.

Bibliography: Hypnosis

Amen, Daniel G. *Change Your Brain, Change Your Life: The Breakthrough Program for Conquering Anxiety, Depression, Obsessiveness, Anger and Impulsiveness*. New York: Crown, 1999.

Blair, Forbes Robbins. *Instant Self-Hypnosis: How to Hypnotize Yourself with Your Eyes Open*. Naperville, Ill.: Sourcebooks, 2004.

Burke, Adam. *Self-Hypnosis: New Tools for Deep and Lasting Transformation*. Berkeley: Crossing Press, 2004.

Edgette, John and Tim Rowan. *Winning the Mind Game: Using Hypnosis in Sports Psychology*. Bancyfelin, Carmarthen: Crown House, 2003.

Gafner, George and Sonja Benson. *Handbook for Hypnotic Inductions*. New York: Norton, 2000.

Goldberg, Bruce. *Self-Hypnosis: Easy Ways to Hypnotize Your Problems Away*. Franklin Lakes, N.J.: New Page, 2001.

Hadley, Josie and Carol Staudacher. *Hypnosis for Change*. Oakland: New Harbinger, 1996.

Hathaway, Michael R. *The Everyday Hypnosis Book*. Avon, Mass.: Adams Media, 2003.

Hewitt, William W. *Hypnosis for Beginners: Reach New Levels of Awareness and Achievement*. St. Paul: Llewellyn, 1986.

Hewitt, William W. *Self-Hypnosis for a Better Life*. St. Paul: Llewellyn, 2004.

Liggett, Donald. *Sport Hypnosis*. Champaign, Ill.: Human Kinetics Publishers, 2000.

LeCron, Leslie M. *Self-Hypnotism: The Technique and Its Use in Daily Living*. New York: Penguin, 1970.

Mycoe, Stephen. *Unlimited Sports Success: The Power of Hypnosis*. Lincoln, Nebr.: Writers Club, 2001.

Streeter, Michael. *Hypnosis: Secrets of the Mind*. Hauppauge, N.Y.: Barron's, 2004.

Temes, Roberta. *The Complete Idiot's Guide to Hypnosis*. 2nd ed. New York: Alpha, 2004.

Tolle, Eckhart. *The Power of Now*. Novato, Calif.: New World Library, 2004.

Vanzant, Iyanla. *Until Today!* New York: Simon Schuster, 2000.

Walsch, Neale Donald. *Conversations with God*. Thorndike, Maine: Thorndike, 1997.

We hope that you have enjoyed this little book about the game of Life, i.e., Golf. For greater improvement, consider seeing a hypnotherapist in your area for personal guidance. If you would like to purchase a set of CDs or tapes that will enable you to change your brain and change your game, please contact:

The Holmes Center for Hypnotherapy
639 North Larchmont Blvd., Suite # 107
Los Angeles, California 90004 USA

Phone: 323-817-8888

Website: www.holmeshypnotherapy.com

E-mail: drwholmes@aol.com

The cost of the set is $125.00 US, plus shipping and handling.

James Walter Caufield is a freelance journalist living in Los Angeles. His latest project is a self-help book for nature lovers.

Dr. Wanita Holmes: Hypnotherapist, lecturer, teacher and author. Dr. Wanita Holmes is known internationally in the field of hypnotherapy. Dr. Holmes has been doing hypnotherapy for eighteen years and has been teaching for twelve years. Her style of teaching and doing hypnotherapy is warm, compassionate and life changing.